An Intimate Guided Tour

Places In God

by
Beryle E. Whitten

authorHOUSE®

AuthorHouse™
1663 Liberty Drive
Bloomington, IN 47403
www.authorhouse.com
Phone: 1 (800) 839-8640

First Published by AuthorHouse 06/17/2007
Published by AuthorHouse 02/07/2017

ISBN: 978-1-4208-6105-1 (sc)
ISBN: 978-1-4634-9826-9 (e)

Print information available on the last page.

Scripture quotations marked KJV are from the Holy Bible, King James Version
(Authorized Version). First published in 1611. Quoted from the KJV Classic
Reference Bible, Copyright © 1983 by The Zondervan Corporation.

Dedication

To Rosa Waddell

As our ships passed going in different directions, I turned mine around to follow yours through the Straits of Commitment on the Sea of Seriousness. I sailed alongside your vessel and requested permission to come aboard. I learned from you how to loosen things that are tight, how to eliminate squeaks and how to shine that which is dull. I used your spiritual oil. Its viscosity holds. You have a simple truth, a generous spirit and humility, all gifts from God that a lesser person would exploit. As I disembark, may I dedicate this work to you?

Acknowledgements

Who but God?

My expanding appreciation goes to the Still Small Voice who dictated every word of this work.

There were people who were major parts of the scaffolding needed to protect and access my development. Some of them knew how the finished product would be. Some were removed before the framework was to come down. The strongest and most daring influence on me was the late Ms. Hall, my pet name for my mother. She had access to the blueprint and she knew destiny had dug the foundation.

To my father, the late Frank Spires, who secured the footers for the pouring of the cement, I owe deep appreciation.

Neighbors and teachers were parts of the scaffolding. I say thank you to those people who met me in God's perfection to promote His plan.

I want to acknowledge the late Valerie J. Johnson who translated my longhand original from a legal pad to a hard drive.

I thought it was a hard drive. She assured me it was an easy trip. She was confident this work would be published.

Pamala Murphy, M.D. did a fine tooth combing of the manuscript early on to check for systemic anomalies.

Thank you, also, to Ruby Connor-Wade, Ph.D., who helped me to switch from "Caution" to "Go".

Lots of hugs and kisses go to Ernest L. Fann, a playwright of the finest sort. He is skilled with uniqueness and has an uncanny ability to plot and describe characters with breathtaking alarm. His valued input gave me strong direction.

This work would still be in a large plastic bag, with strong handles, if it were it not for Darlene K. Willis. Her talents, energies, time and kindness, I hold in careful esteem and for which I am enormously grateful.

Congratulations to the congregants of Spiritual Growth Ministries. They were tremendously encouraging, patient and tolerant. They endured me and my eternal book without complaint (that I could hear).

And to my "Bera" (Vera Barnhill) who, from day one has insisted, "One day I will walk into a major bookstore and see a title authored by Beryle E. Whitten. Every time I go, I look. I know it will be there." From deep, deep down in my being I champion her and thank her for believing those things I could not see.

I send a strong, very personal thank you to those companies and agents and people who rejected this manuscript. Each one layered my determination. I saw each of them seated inside

God, in my theatre, waiting to become an actor in the screenplay of my life. I needed them and they were there.

I acknowledge George. He had a silent knowing that had every confidence in me and in my eternal book. He found and nurtured a "me" I did not know. His encouraging gentleness and steadfastness held me steady and on course for over forty years of marriage. He died before the eternal book was in print in the natural. He watched it unfold in real life. Thanks, George. Now you can read it without your glasses.

Contents

Foreword

Imagine being inside of God's ear and hearing all the prayers, all the languages spoken in the world. Imagine walking on shiny red embroidery threads that are the heart strings of God. At one point, there is a six wheeled bus driven by each passenger from one area to another. Each is transported by thought, led by a Phoenix and instructed by the Major Angel.

Places in God is an allegorical journey that will find a permanent home in your heart and in your library.

Introduction

I taught a home based Bible study group in which we explored several aspects of God, as we knew Him. We studied the process of shepherding sheep. We used Phillip Keller's <u>A Shepherd Looks at Psalm 23</u> as a text book. After learning about the tedious work done by the shepherd to keep and control a flock of sheep, we compared that journey to the Song of Solomon. The difference was in functioning as a unit as compared to responding individually in a personal relationship.

The comparison revealed ideas about God that had two things in common: First, God was perceived as a holy magician that needed to be appeased, friendly, yet not too reliable for answering prayer requests. Answers were most times off in the future of maybe or in the sweet by and by. Moreover, the God the class knew existed outside, up in Heaven. Second, the idea that we really did not <u>know</u> God become apparent. We discovered that the old time religion held us captive. Our study revealed some facts about who God was not.

Phillip Keller's study of the 23rd Psalm gave us clear insight into the hard work necessary for maintaining sheep "for His namesake." That was the focal point that established the reason for the shepherd's investment in the sheep.

During that year we trudged along as an imaginary flock of sheep through sleet and snow, through the early spring storms into summer, to cool, grassy table lands where the lambs could romp and play.

The transformation from sheep to beloved took place in the Song of Solomon. It was not noticeable at first. We began to see ourselves as individuals with singular relationships with God first, then with each other. We became marvelously aware of ourselves.

We had serious difficulties in our families: unemployment, divorce and a new house construction in which the builder declared bankruptcy. Out of that trouble, unity emerged. It was solid and single. I called it our Phoenix.

The imaginary bird invited us to follow it. Each followed at a speed and direction peculiar to her own perception. There were five of us.

What is offered here is an account of one personal journey; a guided tour inside God's body.

Obedience

The first stop was The Place of Obedience which was an inward part that is not hidden. It is an area where there is a transformation that concludes the former life.

As they followed the bird they were approaching a building that was in full view because they were far away from it. The closer they got, the bigger it was. When they went through the entrance, they lost all concept of the size of the outside. Their attention was involved with the inside. They were so impressed with the outside they assumed the inside. When that happens people will express their personal prejudices and miss God altogether – so busy with the outside.

Obedience is a Place in God where your insides are tempered with the fire of "Just Do It." The concept of learning obedience is a misnomer. It is like jump rope for children at play, movement, but no progress. Why spend time trying to learn something you already know? With God, the issue is not "should you?" but "will you?"

Obedience is not learned, it is just remembered. Obedience is not a hard taskmaster; it is a Place to say yes because you believe His Truth. In Him, there is no demanding rhetoric, no" on the mark, get set, go!" Either you do or not. If not, you will always stay in the Place of Obedience– motion but no advancement.

The phoenix was breath taking in its beauty. It had electric colors of violet and green with deep yellow tuck feathers mixed into its great wings. Its eyes were bright transparent warm glass, set deep in its round head. The bird announced that they were to follow it. It spoke English, only in bird language, which each of them understood. They followed.

The Obedience area was open and wide. There, they were to leave off the outer parts of their inward beings. The transformation would eliminate the idea that they were all body. It would make them aware of the God part of them, inside and out.

There was loveliness in the words they heard, "*I Am the God for whom you have been seeking. You want to know why, you want to know when. You have put time and energy in trying to study about Me. You have learned what men say about Me. They taught you about My outside. Come inside and taste and see. Your troubles brought you here to this time and Place inside Me. Remember, you did not choose Me, I chose you. Now follow on to know that I Am God.*"

Yieldedness

As the Phoenix fluttered and moved on in Him it led Beryle to the Place of Yieldedness. It was a large lobby resplendent with grand paintings and murals. All the walls were glowing in hues of deep purple and sparkling gold. There were huge stones in places that identified patterns. The walls expanded and moved as her gaze followed them from one direction clockwise. She stood and stared. The floor was moving slowly to suggest that she should move. Even though the movement of the floor was without noise or motion, it caused her to be moved, though she stood still. A cloud-like silence enclosed around her and she had neither size nor dimension. She became an integral part of the inside of God.

The inner walls were an unbelievable magnificence of objects and hanging coverings. There were molded figures in undeserved prettiness. Orderly quiet whispers filled the Place. Slowly she became aware she was inside of God. Her understanding went numb. She began to understand things she already knew and had not thought. She knew there was a giving up, a painless surrendering of the person who had arrived. It just happened.

She was willing to trade everything she knew (everything is not much inside of God) for all she did not know. She was trading for the unsearchable riches of the mysteries of God, hidden for those who would yield. That perception would have caused some excitement in her but the element was somehow absent or non-functioning. She just settled into a willingness to yield.

When God made man His intent was to see Himself in the man. He wanted to see a projection of Himself in man's resplendent glory. Man was on an assignment to groom and care for the earth as he enjoyed his wife and children. Such plans still remain.

When you arrive at the Place of Yieldedness there is no discussion about wrong and right. Your personal self is dealt with in that area. Gains and losses are balanced on the scale of "what is". When the scale comes to full stop you will have to determine that which ought to be. You can get off the scale. The personal self is weighed against God's desire for the good and right way.

Obedience, persuaded by Truth, will cause you to sidestep determinations. That is Yieldedness – the willingness to "want to" through surrendered availability.

All Truth

The movement of the floor ushered her into the Place of All Truth. It was pristine clean, clear, no pictures, no images. It was bright with happy music. The walls were stern brass, glass, and marble. There were large, tall white sticks standing from the floor like soldiers. They presented a labyrinth, intricate and elaborate. If any of the sticks was in the wrong place or was not of truth the stick would fall down. There was room in between the sticks like pathways. They did not touch the non-existing ceiling (which looked like fluffy clouds). They would all fall if one fell.

Do lies work like that? In the Place of All Truth a person is given to know truth. She asked God about the Place and how it related to knowing truth.

"The labyrinth is a skill selector. It increases with probability as you desire and divulge truth. When you have an honest conception you give birth to freedom. The freedom is released by your desire to do right.

7

"You will come to know there are no rules in your new found freedom. You will want to cooperate with My Righteousness. Your arrival at this Place was voluntary and it made you increase. While you are learning My insides, your dimensions decrease. There is so much more of Me than of you. As I increase, you decrease. This Place has nothing to do with knowledge as you perceive it. All Truth just is. It rings loud bells and tells tales of itself to you in your heart. It keeps you knowing. It flows out of itself into itself.

"This Place is bound by your belief system. How much of All Truth do you believe? Over what part do you stumble? If you need to know why you cannot believe a truth, it is because you will not make room inside your belief system for it. You will not delete the old. Some people die here. They take on the colors of their old belief patterns and become parts of the wall hangings in the outer lobby – In Him, in the Yieldedness lobby.

"Many of the tapestries you saw on the walls were people who died in the Place of All Truth because of their belief processes – which they refused to change. They are in Me but stuck to a wall.

"<u>Truth is not variable; it does not become untruth because you do not believe it.</u> Make sure you filter everything you believe through this truism. Say this to yourself when you permit doubt to challenge you in the arena of your own understanding."

The Place of the Christ Mind

Her attention was attracted by a warm, loud swoosh. The bird was moving to the Place of the Christ Mind. She was invited to browse. She was told any expectation existing in her head would be reflected in that Place. It was resplendent with mirrors – all she saw were images of her.

"Is this the Mind of Christ?"

"A desire to understand operates in you at all times. This area is a Board room for you to meet with your will, your intellect and your emotions. The Christ Mind room is always reserved just for you."

"What about the others?"

"Is there any limit of space in Me? I have ordained this journey for you to lead others. Your teachings are guided tours through Me.

"The Christ Mind is not an object it is a Place in Me. For reflective observation and purposeful judgment, you need a Place to think things through. It is like being in a library just to get away. The quiet cleans out your ears. Books are not on

shelves here, they are thought waves. In this Place you think a thought and it finds its components, then it feeds itself back into your mind, the way images bounce off mirrors only faster.

*"The Place of the Christ Mind is the **just** place in Me where you are free to arbitrate. You are free to select, identify and to plug into fantasy; to pawn dreams and trade. This venue offers a selection of ideas, goals, accomplishments and things and stuff for you to bounce around. You can even play with them. You can ponder, meditate or just sit and look. Surely you would want to get a cart and take some ideas with you."*

In Him

There was neither time nor space In Him. The only dimensions she noticed were those put there by her and by her own concept of separation and seclusion. She thought, *This part is His mouth and this part is His throat,* - from where she could see into His ears. It was all transparent and just a thought took her up or down and caused her to see right through His insides.

"God, where am I now?"

"You are inside of Me."

"Did I need to know anything about being in You before I got here?"

"Of course you needed to know everything you know. That is what brought you here."

"Could You have zapped me here?"

"Not a chance! That would have defeated My purpose and it would have cheated all the people you had to meet along the way. Do you remember a small lady who bought one of your books in St. Louis at the Holy Spirit Conference (as I recall they

called it an Explosion)? She told you she saw you as a tree with a trunk so large she could not get her arms around it?

"Remember another lady who thanked you for obeying the Holy Spirit? To quote her, 'I know the Holy Spirit wrote your book, I recognize His handwriting.' Some of those books went to Japan, Germany, Brazil, Puerto Rico, Nassau, Hawaii and places East, West, North and South from those places. Who would have written your book? Who would have written this one? No, I do not zap.

"To be In Him is designed to marinate you. It is to soak your skin in spiritual formaldehyde (a colorless pungent gas used as a preservative and disinfectant). Come on, stretch! You need to be coated and treated with a protective sealant to keep you in all your ways. Now your ways are no longer your ways, but My ways. When you are being led by Spirit along the lighted paths you need protection.

"In Spirit, the attacks come from front and rear. Some attacks come with noise and fury and some with sneak and stealth. This Place in Me is a Place of 'rest in soak'. It is where you are scanned for flaws and cracks. My sensors survey your intent, your heart and your nervous system. Your hearing is tested frequently. I screen and re-screen for visual and mental acuity. I search and find all sorts of things in this Place. It is not that I do not know where they are, you do not know. This is a breakout room, a little off the beaten path. You might want to know why there is no crowd here. Many people never get past the Christ Mind. They like the variety and busyness in there.

"IN HIM IS SERIOUS.

"It is a preparation Place for things to come. Your journey from here will be without script or purse; no road map, no advanced notice of directional change. It is a good idea to begin the count in this Place.

"In Him is the Place to count the cost. It is an exchange booth – a Place to exchange what you have for what you will need."

The Place of the Pure Heart

The heart is usually thought of as the source of romance and love. The loveliness of that Place exceeds the others because of its purity. Inside of God is all goodness, which decries description. The Place of the Pure Heart is the source of the throb of energy. There electricity is generated to motivate one to keep seeking and to keep being lured.

The five students were watching for the Phoenix. It hovered over a large cloud-like arrangement of white fluffy vastness. There had been no sudden movement since they came inside of God, yet the Place was pulsating like a heartbeat. Motion sounds, soothing rhythmic elastic ideas swirled around in space inviting them to get involved. There were no dimensions, no limits, no form, just space and ideas; they were ribbons of information. As airy as they seemed, they were solid with mass.

An extremely gummy, pasty substance was attached to the ribbons. As they waved and floated near her they engulfed her. It did not hurt nor was it sticky. It was absorbed into her body.

She began to pulsate and beat. Each band probed her self-ness – as if looking for that which was impure. They found ideas, fears, don'ts, shame, half-hearted thank yous, worn out dreams and introductions. The ribbons of purity were coated with silken Teflon. As they engaged what they found, the illusionary images were gently swept in the direction outside her self – to be screened by her ego to see if she wanted to keep them.

God said, *"If you keep them they will be reflected in what you teach."*

The teacher had never seen a real Phoenix (that is to say she had not seen one in the real world and since it is not a real bird in the first place, you know why she had never seen one. That one had led her inside of God and she saw it). The Phoenix began to flap its wings and cry and screech and sing all at the same time. There was no noise, no movement, only the throbbing pulsing indication of the beating Heart of God inside the Place of the Pure Heart.

Beryle did not want to miss this. Her thought was to remain here and rest because of the movement and of the energetic activity of the ribbons. She decided to twirl around and play with them to see if she could shake loose some of the isms they found. As she twirled she heard Him say, **"Be still and know that I am God."**

That did it. She wanted to go. Maybe her twirling was inappropriate. She felt too close; not sure too close to what.

Have you ever been there in the Place of the Pure Heart, where hearts are changed? Can you see why the beating never

15

stops? (No pun intended). The things released will cause an enlarged heart. They will quiet the systolic mummer of the religious infestation so common among people.

The Phoenix was quieter as it whispered, *"Do not leave, you have come this far – you must see the next Place – nothing can compare. For your whole journey, the next Place will prove to be the Pearl of Great Price. You will want to buy the whole field."*

The place where her heart used to be was an enlarged hollow chamber of emotion. It was soft emotion like that which she felt when she hugged a small toddler. Love flowed from her in soft waves of warm oneness, so lovely – and the pulsing was gone.

There was a slow, ever so slow, movement of Energy behind her. She watched two giant hands lace fingers together to form a colossal, translucent, white French door.

It had templates of turquoise and violet shades of iridescence, much like fish scales that change colors as the creature moves. They were solid massive, stately great doors. As the Phoenix flew towards them they opened – very, very slowly, they opened a distance away from her. As they parted, a blinding streak of warm bright light flooded the hollow heart of God. It bounced off what would be the back wall of God's heart and consumed her.

The Point of No Return

The warm light did not hurt her eyes. It caused her to remember. She was talking to herself out loud or maybe not:

I remember having seen that light once before in the early 1960's when I went to Europe on a fashion tour. There were twenty-one of us. I was a model traveling with fashion designers. I met two ladies on the plane and we became a laughing unit. They were bright, educated and clever. We pooled our resources and our wits. We managed to have a blast of a good time. They made my heart explode with living. We called ourselves the Damon and Pythias group – vowing friendship forever.

After Europe, I went to Los Angeles to visit them and I learned they were Hindu. They invited me to the Hindu temple. That was okay, I went. The thing was for us to sit in silence for a few hours while everyone chanted and said some phrases. Shortly, I was bored. I could see out of an open window. I began to keep count of the cars going in each direction. Soon I began to try to count them by colors and numbers. I cannot say how long I did that.

I do remember having seen that same bright, warm light. I had been sitting and had closed my eyes when the bright light began to gather in the corners of my eyes. It expanded in the shapes of triangles towards the center of my head until my whole head was filled with it. I would have closed my eyes, but they were already closed.

I saw a large, meat-looking image that favored a Volkswagen standing upright on its front end. It looked like a brain with inroads, crevices and wrinkles. It was maroon in color like liver and covered with debris. There were small twigs and bits of glass and what appeared to be ashes (from burned coal).

I was aware of something major going on with me – very, very aware but not quite sure what. When I saw this big round thing I figured it was my "sin sick soul". I do not know if I spoke out loud or if I thought it – I spoke with determined insistence, "I don't want that, take it away!"

The scene changed in an instant. My "sin sick" soul disappeared.

What happened next, words will not help here.

*I saw the '****Love of God****.' I knew '****Truth****'!!!*

I cannot do any better than that. A peace came over me that caused every single cell in my body to wake up to a new electric awareness.

Something overwhelmed my insides. There was a knowing explosion. It was like I knew that I know, now. How do you say you are suddenly infused with God? That was the" Now of God"taking up residence in my insides.

I heard Damon call my name. It was time to go. We were going to a party but I could not go. When she asked why, I said, "My soul is out." I remember not being willing to talk about what happened. I just knew I could not go.

When I got back home, my mother noticed something different about me with the proverbial, "I just can't put my hands on it" – I knew.

That was the Point of No Return. God, Himself, found me in a Hindu temple with my temporary intent to become a Hindu (I had on knee boots, hot pants and earrings big as hubcaps). He made no exception for my dress. Somewhere deep inside of me I knew I had become. What – I was not sure. I just knew. Moreover, I knew I would never return to the metamorphic castoff I left in the Hindu temple one spring evening of perfect weather.

Silence crept into my being and covered my yearning spirit with a handsome sense of peace. It began a unifying of all the parts in preparation for wholeness. Of course, I was fragmented – isn't everyone? As I look back I can see God's signature on that experience. It labeled me.

All at once they each arrived at the Point of No Return – in the inside of God. Each took a turn talking about what she sensed about herself and how the suddenness of Light had impacted her.

The experience left them awestruck. There they were taking a tour of God's insides and were touched in the face with warm brilliant Light. Each one felt the same sensation of being breathless, yet breathing, as if she were infiltrated – yes, that is it. They were absorbed by the Light into Itself. They became the Light that will never go out (pun intended).

A Place Called Allness

When they came to the Allness Place they were aware of being aware. Perhaps it was a Spiritual awakening! Being there was a requirement for release. As long as they were satisfied with whatever existed, with what they already believed and knew, they would have remained <u>sealed in conformity</u>. Passivity would keep them following those who did not know God, and would subsequently keep them from ever knowing Him. There would be no chance for them to evolve into the freedom to know and believe Truth. Therefore, their spirits had to grow past physical confines, to that which would permit such spiritual growth.

You said, "When a man hungers and thirsts after righteousness, he would be filled." What is "filled?" Beryle asked.

"Here it means included. When a man is filled he is included with the filling. All the ingredients used in the filling become a part of him. He assimilates the filler substance and the substance

is distributed on demand. The filler is whole and joins the parts to become part of the whole.

"Imagine a bakery with every ingredient in the backroom to make all the products in the showcases. Each item, though different, is the same. When ingredients are put together they make baked goods. Even though the filler in a doughnut is not dough – it becomes part of the doughnut – included – and will be consumed, too.

"Your spirit grows into the fullness of the physical being and absorbs (if you will) the physical being into itself."

"God, if that is so, where does the power come from to make that happen? How can Spirit overcome the physical?"

"It happens slowly when you work on your willingness to investigate your belief systems and to change them."

"That will take forever."

"You have forever – and what else is there?

"The world, per-se, is not in here yet and it will not get into this Place if someone of you is not brave enough to join those who have led others here: Lao-Tzu, Tagore, Robert Blake (1757-1829), Neville Goddard (1905-1972), Jerry (1954-2015) and Esther Hicks, Wayne Dyer (1940-2015), Deepak Chopra and Neale Donald Walsh.

"People use 'all' everyday with no thought of it being A Place in God."

When one son stayed home and resented his younger brother for having returned – the older took it out on the father – *"What means this thing – you gave him a party and here's me – I stayed here – didn't go off dancing with the wolves and he did. Now he comes waltzing in here and you expect me to be glad to see this stinky person?"* (Loose interpretation) The father summed the older son's supposition with His Allness. (Luke 15: 29-31)

Allness is a Place in God where all of the above originated. It can be a little All or a big All or a welcome All or a missing All. When you get there, sit a while to rest because you are becoming full. Just look around to see what His Allness looks like.

To discover Allness merely requires you to allow Spirit to overtake your little self.

A Point of Excellence

Sometimes, when Beryle wanted to relax, she would stop in a "Nearly New Shop." It was good because no one bothered to try to sell her anything. She would pull through stuff until her heavy purse made her shoulder tired.

One day she heard God say, *"Give some of your clothes away."*

She went through her closet, gathered some of her treasures from the Goodwill and took them to a pretty lady who taught Sunday school. She thought Ms. Flowers would be stunning in front of her class that included the surveying eyes of her female students.

When she returned home, God said, *"Now give away some of your pretty clothes."*

Her first thought was, *Surely you jest!*

He explained that if she frequented the Goodwill, bought Goodwill that would be what she gave away. *"Your gifts are a reflection of Me. I am **Excellent**, **Extravagant** and **Expensive**.*

Stay out of those places. Shop first class, pay full price, you do not have to hunt bargains, I can afford you."

As they moved along in the anatomy of God they turned a corner and discovered they had passed a Place tucked away beyond the glamour; there was no excitement, no announcement. It had the flavor of an exclusive, upscale restaurant with white velvet table cloths, succulent plush carpet and a string quintet.

Their having missed His Excellence as an item, reminded them that they should be more aware of where they were and what was being shown to them. They discussed the idea at length. They were fascinated by the class and exclusivity of that close, intimate Place. They tried to be embarrassed and use the discussion as a way of trying to make up for having missed His Excellence.

Valerie had experienced God's Excellence. Her former husband had been unwilling to pay support for their two young children who were grown and busy parenting. After being away from her home for a week, Valerie was looking through her mail and found three unfamiliar envelopes. The children's father had taken money to the child support bureau and paid it as back support for the two children after twenty two years.

When Beryle and George were building their Murphy's Law house, the builder went bankrupt when the house was two thirds finished. He was kind to them and did not include their house in his bankruptcy. He held their hands and helped them to finish the house. However, they had to pay more money for the things that were included in the original construction loan – totaling $45,000.

Long before they started the process she had prayed for a house, a wooded lot, her own deer, squirrels, rabbits, chipmunks, birds and privacy. She wanted to live in the woods but not in the country. At one prayer point, as she was going down her list God said, *"I cannot give you a house."*

"Why?"

"You do not think big enough!"

"What do you want me to think?"

"Think thousands." That sounded to her like a whispered smile.

She could do that! *Thousands, ten thousands, fifty thousands, one hundred thousands, six hundred thousands,* she thought. That was about as far as she could think, realistically, without thinking much beyond that would be too much.

They got the house finished, moved in and converted the construction loan at 8.5% variable. Mr. Barthany, the loan officer, said, "Check with me in three years and we'll see what the Feds are up to then." Two years went by; interest rates were down. People from mortgage companies had begun to call her offering services and products. Beryle felt comfortable refusing them because she and George had Mr. Barthany to help them when they went to spy on the Feds.

One day in early October, 1998, the phone rang and a deep, sexy male voice asked if they had a "variable".

Something in her spirit clicked "Yes."

"I can help you."

"Fine, when?"

The First Capital Mortgage Company sent an associate to their house. They spoke of interest rates, surveyors, appraisers, cars, chickens, wallpaper, mutual funds and greeting cards. He stayed two hours to conduct fifteen minutes worth of business. He called the next day and said the transaction would close on October 28, 1998, and it did. On that date the interest rate was 6.25% fixed, the lowest it had been since Pat joined the army.

Here is the <u>excellent bonus</u>. They figured the difference between the two interest rates on the loans. The 6.25% fixed loan was $48,000 less than the 8.5% loan. How excellent was that?

The Place of the Single Eye

The Phoenix had a directional pull that caused them to move along. They could still see the enormously bright light that engulfed each of them. As a unit, they resembled a giant balloon bobbing along. Overhead, a huge shadow of a ball appeared, like a slow moving cloud. An orbit engulfed it to cause the appearance of an eye. Was that the Seeing Eye?

God said, *"No – it is the SINGLE EYE. It is the source of body light.*

"My yoke is easy and My burden is light. It is the yoke of hooking up with Me to be lit. I could be your electric illuminating company. The idea is for your eye to become single to aspects of Me. Have the courage to disclose your need of the freedom found in Me and My light.

"A new phase of your existence is evolving. Here is the Place to look at and let go of the ideas of failures, mistakes and sufferings. Everyone makes mistakes and suffers. It is called missing the mark. But missing the mark can be overcome by banishing the great ignorance that causes it."

"What great ignorance?"

"It is called the Ignorance of unbelief."

"What should I believe – or better yet – what should I not believe?"

"'Should' does not enter here. Believe it all or believe none of it until you process the information. Traditions, experiences, and dogmas, have been presented to you. You used some of them to establish your belief systems. Developmental aging is not the issue, acceptance is the issue. What you accept defines what you choose to believe.

"If I say, 'I am light' you might believe I said it. If you do not accept it – My light will not exist for you – though you know light exists. If you heard that the very substance of My light is healing power and you rejected the possibility of that power – even though the light remains a factor in your belief systems, you could not produce the healing.

"Your eye becomes single when you and I become one. When you absorb the light and are absorbed by the light, then your eye becomes single to My Magnificence. There cannot be a space between you and Me. If there is, it will be filled with you, your ego, and your self-will from which will come self-effort. This division or separateness establishes the 20/20 vision that causes you to see yourself as God, and Me as god. When your eye becomes single, you will be yourself in God – unified.

"As you begin to see this unity, the ideas of My perfection will come clear to you. You will come to know that there is no lack or suffering in Me. The blending of thoughts and ways will

generate the vision that becomes single. Think of looking at one thing at a time."

She had to think about the eye. She thought of the power of All-ness, and of how All was shrunk into one word, one idea, one "is" at a time – one "now." Translate that one, to a single vision looking at one thing. Through one single channel, light will flood and fill the body. *That seems reasonable*, she thought.

The Phoenix told them to leave the past behind, release it with joy and take up their new lives to live in the Great Eternal Now.

The Now of God

Suddenly, the Phoenix gave a mighty flap and flew around and around her, causing her body to wiggle and shake. The shaking caused her body to come apart at her joints. Her skin, (the thick gummy stuff) held her together. The Phoenix hovered over her and fanned its wings, in a fashion that was almost apologetic. It was a soothing gentle motion that was re-minding her (as in re-wiring her mind). Her joints went back together and she was whole again. In spite of that action there was no pain, no idea of discomfort. Maybe it felt like a good strong welcome stretch. She just stood there, amazed and glad and reconnected.

Gradually, her full attention was drawn to the Place where they were. The Phoenix announced it:

A Place called Now.

They just stood there staring. There were two pieces of furniture.

There was a large, overstuffed chaise with rolled up arms. Each end housed a soft fluffy pillow. The sides were free like a day bed.

Beryle sat down on it. The thought crossed her mind, was she sitting on the Now? Questions about that Place floated in and out of her awareness. They would dissolve because Now was all she had and she was sitting on it. The questions were about the past and the future. They were dissolved before they were formulated.

She thought about the time God told her thoughts were "alphabet carriers" that hovered over her waiting for her to speak words. He said the words spoken would break up into alphabets and these carriers would then reduce them to common denominators. They would carry the spoken words into the Universe to cause what she said to come to pass. The idea seemed so fabulous to her that she wanted to teach it. She wanted to make some kind of visible prototype to use as demonstration. Now she knew the visible prototype was unnecessary. All she had to do was to speak. In the Place of God's Now the words become active.

As she thought about that, her attention was drawn to a large, shelved, glass display case across from the Now. It was the other piece of furniture in the place.

In it were hand crafted ceramic horses, majestic glass eagles, a small child, and a mature woman. One glorious, transparent swan was floating on a small water circle that glistened as the swan moved. There was a little clock shaped like a wheel that turns an old pirate ship. There were no numbers, the words NOW pronounced the time.

The huge glass case had three separate sections joined together to make one unit. In the center shelf space in unit two, there was a masterpiece limited edition of sculptured clowns, including a court jester. They had tasseled hats; leggings striped with brightly colored ribbons, knee stockings, and pointed toe shoes with pompoms. Handsome colors attracted attention to each item of clothing. Strangely, when she looked at them, they began to move and dance and sing. They bowed and made gestures, clapped their hands and giggled. One very young clown-in-training had a small sign, large enough for him to lean on. As he walked about, the writing on the sign scrolled in various languages, most were foreign to her brain, but her spirit could read some of them:

...This is now bone of my bones, and flesh of my flesh... *(Genesis 2:23)*

...and now nothing will be restrained from them, which they have imagined to do. (Genesis 11:6)

The giant units were encased with large, rounded glass doors.

When she looked at the eagles they would pose perched with their wings spread. Their feathers were spangled with musical colors that harmonized strength and protection, with the gentle ease of a whispered swoosh. The eagles were on the shelf above the clowns. As the clowns moved about, the eagles just sat there with their wings fanning open, protecting the busy characters. They were unaware of their gifts of protection.

There were four tiers to each section. The creatures and people were spaced in individual places. Under the clowns, in the center section was a huge horse's head made of tiny triangular mirrors. Its head was black with a full gray mane that dazzled, as did large brownish- beige eyes. Nostril veins scooped from the nose that helped the mouth to stay open. It was a wide mouth empty of teeth and tongue – just mouth.

She noticed a glaring red rose, lower left shelf, with a young girl staring at it. The flower seemed to be growing; no movement, just evolving and changing the shapes of the petals. The rose was half the height of the child; the changing of the petals created movement of her flowing skirt.

The highest level on the right side housed a brown velvet eagle, in flight – not far from an amber colored egg. Under them on the second level, was an elaborate, skillfully carved miniature Emmett Kelley clown, playing a small violin. He was near the place where a beautiful black baby swan swam on a tiny mirror. This gave new meaning to Swan Lake. The violin music embodied and embraced the mind waves of celebrated classical composers. It would not be fair to say she studied each item individually. In her mind she took a picture of the essence of each single image and knew.

Under the eagle and the amber colored egg was an Indian, clad in a loincloth, astride a falling horse. The position of the stumbled horse pronounced sure death to the Indian. Agonizing disaster was spilled on the face of the animal. She could see the right arm, shoulder, ribs and legs of the man. His head was curled forward under his neck. He was soon to roll forward onto his back off the horse. The horse's body was upright with his left foreleg, full out under him. His head and his neck were on the ground. His tail was poised for balance, his left hind leg was folded in a trot posture, and the other leg was straight. They were in the air – there was no movement. That was a stop screen image that just stood there.

Between the stark Indian on the horse was an elegant, carved vase connected to a square base that sat on four large marbles. It was ice blue glass with four fan images etched on the bowl. Its shape was that of an open tulip – with scallops around the top that rose and fell to distinguish a petal pattern in the edge of the vase mouth. Etching gave it a cool refreshing inviting openness. It sat alone in the large space that was under the horse's head, made of small black and gray triangular mirrors.

Left of the horse was a shapely, slim woman made of powdered marble dust. In spite of her being made of marble, her image was soft and warm. She was smiling at a small flower she held in her right hand. She looked as though she had dismounted a shiny Gobel horse that had thick legs and square hooves – no saddle.

In the same chamber with the gold ship's wheel, there was a porcelain horse in motion running so fast that all four feet were in the air. – "Fast Flight Flee" he whinnied. That motion caused the tiny gold ship's wheel clock to tick, as if trying to catch the porcelain horse.

To the left of the two white eagles was the same young animal in a position of STOP. Perhaps it was a quarter horse. It was standing still – yet in a motion mode.

Under the stunning young animal was a crystal four-leaf clover next to a horse head, carved from a piece of parasitic wood that grew on a Bayberry tree. Neck mane, head, ears, eyes, open mouth, and throat veins all fade into a flowering scarred piece of damaged wood. The sore was made when the parasitic wood was pulled from its host.

Wait, one more thing – a miniature, crystal angel two inches tall, was blowing a tiny trumpet. He had thick sloping wings and skinny arms. There was a precious gold halo; his eyes squinted shut. He was blowing over a miniscule seashell. The seashell was breathing in and out as if to help the angel to blow. Beryle watched the shell as a solid long blast sounded louder and louder. When she looked away, it fell silent. When the blasting fell silent, all the movement in the case stopped.

A strong but gentle voice said, *"All of life is depicted here. From the egg to death, growing, dancing, playing, starting, stopping, rescinding, resting, pretending, risking and gaining. Who among you chooses to jest the court? Each item has a place inside of you NOW."*

The Realm of the Divine Spirit

In God there is neither time nor space – only NOW – She did not know that when she came in. She knew those words academically, but she had become Now. Sitting on NOW (the overstuffed chaise) becoming the live stock of life, she thought, "How *can I be a NOW and how did I become it?" I do not want to miss this."*

God said, *"What is it you do not want? Have you been here so long and have you not known? There is no 'I do not want' in God – in the Realm of the Divine Spirit all systems are 'go'. Is that so hard to believe? You are used to doing things wrong; you are used to making mistakes. There are no such things here.*

"The Realm of the Divine Spirit is not a Place, it is a Where. It is like the difference between lungs, air and breath. They are interdependent, yet separate. Until it is apparent that the Realm of the Divine Spirit is a Where, you will continue to think of Me as separate from you. You must be attached to the All of Me. My IS-NESS is you. Your is-ness is who I AM. Think of awareness – cognition – knowing. When you let Me/God be God in you – that

is when the Realm of the Divine Spirit is activated. It does not do anything – it just is.

"It is a Place of Attitude. You cannot touch an attitude, yet you know it is. You cannot touch space, yet it exists. In the Realm of the Divine Spirit all possibilities develop, take shape, and come into fruition.

"That is why your concept of Me must meld into your concept of you and God verses YOU-GOD. When it is apparent to you that I, God, want what you want, that I AM what you are, then the Realm of the Divine Spirit disappears like breath. Breath only comes in when needed.

"It is knowing you are God. When you know who you are, you do not have to wear a nametag. You only wear a nametag when other people need to know who you are."

The Realm of the Divine Spirit test came at a banquet during a publisher's convention. An executive where Beryle was employed had an extra ticket; she and he went.

She stopped in the lounge to wash her hands before dinner. Open seating made her selection for her. The only vacant seat was at table One. Chief executive officers and newspaper owners were seated there. She was very hungry. With napkin in her lap she started in on the plated salad and asked for the bread. It was halfway through the rubber chicken that she noticed she was the only one at the table eating. One guy took his fork and broke the tip of the pie and pushed it away and poured his leftover watered down drink into his coffee.

When the "push your embarrass button" thought popped into her head she heard the teacher voice inside say, *"You know truth. You know who you are – it makes you free to eat this free food, now enjoy it."*

The Realm of the Divine Spirit is a knowing that lives deep inside. It is a rudder, a landmark, a lighthouse beam. It is an exchange clearinghouse where you exchange dumb stuff for the magnificence of that which you know for certain. Sometimes you have that knowing covered with the cloth of *I might make a mistake – they might think I am greedy –* you know the kind of stuff.

While they were seated on the Chaise of Now, becoming All of Life, They heard God say, a very loud "**<u>Amen!!!</u>**"

Spiritual Growth

When her son, Darryl, was nine years old, he was complaining that his knees and elbows hurt. His mother's first thought was his bicycle. Hot baths and baby oil should fix that right up. After two doctors and no results, Beryle's sister, Dorothy, recommended old Doctor Ward, the neighborhood pediatrician.

After a fun-filled few minutes the kindly pediatrician gave his verbal diagnosis and prescription: "The lad has growing pains. The bones grow at the ends. Sometimes kids grow too fast and it hurts them. Rub him with alcohol then lotion. The rubbing will do more good than the alcohol. The lotion smells good and he'll like that. He'll probably outgrow it before he learns to live with it."

She never forgot the kindly gentle old doctor's wonder wisdom.

Growing pains of the spirit sometimes stop you. All spiritual growth is gradual. It only hurts when it is being forced on too fast or too involved with resisted truth. The truth only hurts when it is supposed to. Sometimes truth shows up as sandpaper people designed to rub you the wrong way. When the same way rubbing occurs it causes shining and finishing. Too much rubbing with the grain can make depressions. What happens when the rubbing is the wrong way?

While she was wondering about all the beautiful images she had seen while she was seated on the comfortable, gorgeous chaise, she had not noticed the chaise was moving.

When the movement attracted her attention she became aware that they were sailing along on what had become a chute. They were moving away from the inside of the Now. They were on a people transport, like in airports.

They were upright riding straight forward on a level surface. They passed images of people, some transparent, others solid. They could see them waiting in lines and formed in groups. Perhaps they passed by you. It was a carefree, high-spirited ride that went around a corner and stopped.

That was strange. It was the first sudden movement; the stopping. They were in a classroom, still on the chaise. There was a place overhead for transparencies and a large board for writing. There were individual desks with attached seats a – la – elementary school. The overhead grand ball of light, that had been following them, broke away into individual entities, each at a desk.

An instructor appeared. Her presence vacuumed the sound out of the room. Beryle was the instructor. Suddenly, she knew. The Place of Spiritual Growth is where questions are asked and the answers are lived out. At that instant her eyes came open and she knew. More light came into her body. Her eye became single to the glory of God's wisdom.

Wow! What took her out about God, was how cool He was and how easily He lead them into All Truth – that is, all the truth they could tolerate then.

Driving too fast one day she had heard God say, *"How fast will this car go?"*

"Speedometer registers 120 miles per hour."

"What is the speed limit?"

"Fifty-five".

"How fast are you going?"

Breaking down, she responded, "Seventy-five."

God answered, ***"You have to pass by right to do wrong."***

When Beryle was in college, she had an assignment to read a collection of children's writings. They were assigned to write a mystery in as few words as possible. The one mystery she never forgot is quoted here: "Needless to talk, said the French Spy".

When God talks, I find it needless for me to comment – unless, of course, I am resisting truth, she thought, as she drove the rest of the way careful to keep the speed limit.

There was the time when she had been invited to speak at a convention out of state. The hostess provided lodging for her at Ms. Davis' home. Beryle knew Ms. Davis and told her she was going to spend time with someone else in the city.

When the event was over the hostess went to pay Beryle by waving an envelope in her face. She was angry to a fault because Beryle did not stay with Ms. Davis.

That was not a good situation for either of them. Beryle took her good time to fill her lungs with air so she would not have to stop to breathe, before she blew that angry woman halfway down the hall.

A strong Voice said, ***"Don't defend yourself!!***

Gently, she eased the air out of her lungs and just stood there. When the hostess realized there was not going to be an argument, she stopped fussing and handed Beryle the envelope. She was scared that if she said anything, it would sound to God like she was trying to defend herself. Carefully, she leaned forward and whispered, "Thank you for telling me that."

About forty miles down the turnpike, crying hot tears, too mad to talk she hollered, "GOD, WHY DIDN'T YOU LET ME DEFEND MYSELF?"

"You can defend yourself when you are fully persuaded that I can't!"

Needless to talk, said the French Spy.

You can tell you are growing when your feet get bigger. How many times have you found your shoes were too little? When your spiritual feet get bigger than your carnal shoes you should not wear them anymore. There is such a thing as outgrowing a system of thought – learning new truths about old ideas.

The high school class reunion committee chairperson called Beryle one day to invite her to be on the program. She said, "I need you to say something crazy. You know how silly you were in high school. I need someone to make the people laugh." The "get insulted" horse began to stamp at the ground of Beryle's feelings. That made her feelings hurt.

The spiritual growth teacher inside said, "Accept."

Her speech went something like this:

I have been put out of almost everything I have ever been in. When I was in kindergarten the teacher gave me some clay. She told me I could make anything I wanted. I asked her three times if I could do that. Then, I asked if the clay were mine and could I have it to take home. She said yes. So I made a bird, a bird's nest and three little eggs. She fired them in a kiln and gave me some paints. I asked again – she said yes, again. This time I asked about the colors for the things I had made. She said to paint them any color I liked. I painted the bird brown on the back and red on the belly; painted the nest brown and the eggs red. The logic was that if a robin's breast were red and she sat on the eggs, they would be red.

Teacher said I had to paint the eggs blue. I told her she had said I could paint them whatever colors I liked; I like red. You said they were mine. I want mine red. I was crying when I hollered at her. She sent me to the Principal's office.

I got put out of the choir in Elementary school. I got put out of cooking class in Junior High school. I got put out of band in Senior High School. I got put out of the library in college. I got put out of Buckingham Palace in London. I have been put out of a hospital, a bank, a church, a prayer group and several relationships. I even got put out of a marriage.

By then the entire audience was laughing. She continued, "*As you know I was a majorette in school. One day I traded my baton for a Bible – I am still marching but I step to a different drum beat – and the best part of the switch is no one can put me out."*

There was a few seconds before the audience realized she was finished. The whole thing did not take more than two minutes – she grew more in those two minutes than she knew. It was a while before she knew her feet did not fit the "be ashamed of your past" shoes any more. In the Realm of the Divine Spirit you can come to grips with your past and permit it to dissolve into God's Now.

If Barbara still had the image of high school silliness when she thought of Beryle – which aspect of God's Excellence told her to invite Beryle to make the people laugh. They laughed, she grew.

There was a time she thought she had to help God. One day she was driving past a park that was divided by a four-lane street. A family of two parents and eight or nine ducklings were crossing the four lanes. "God, please, please don't let the ducks get run over, please, God please." she prayed.

And the precious Voice answered, *"Do I need you to help Me to take care of my birds?"*

Something more serious needed growing.

Their son, one of one, left home one day a very young, fuzzy-faced, lanky, bag of bones, on his way to graduate from high school. Twenty years later he came back. He had been to College, to the US. Navy, he had a professional basketball career in Argentina for 13 years. He had a wife and two children. He came home, sans all of the above.

She had tried to let him go when he went to college. She was in New York City and went in St. Patrick's Cathedral to pray. She thought the god that lived in Cleveland wouldn't mind if she went over his head...so there she was praying, *"God, I give Darryl to You, please take care of him – watch over him- boo hoo hoo hoo."*

Darryl called home from South Carolina when he was in the Navy. His ship had been ordered to Vietnam.

Guess who took to her bed of affliction. She was on fire from the inside. All her blood vessels burned. Tears did not put that fire out. The medical doctor prescribed tranquilizers with the advice to think about what was making her anxious. He told her to see if it were worth putting chemicals in her body. That diversionary tactic worked. When she threw them away she had grown.

Darryl was on a real battleship in the real war. He came home without the proverbial scratch. His mom was dented and banged up from her war. It took a real stretch for her to realize that her private war was unnecessary.

Home from the war and all his travels presented another issue. Here was an adult male with the accompanying adult male baggage that his mother was trying to fit into a fuzzy-faced, lanky, bag of juvenile bones-mold.

Because she did not see him grow into manhood, it was hard for her to make this real. Her attempts to mother him forced their collective growth hormones into shock-waved overtime. He wanted to love her on his terms.

"Her impeccable love for him was beyond suspicion." – said the French Spy.

That seemed to be a brick wall. She cried and prayed and talked and tried to trick him into letting her control him. He resisted with a sweet passivity. That was his nature. He was respectful, but determined. He never told her to give him a break, although he had every reason. After all, he was grown.

George would constantly remind Beryle that one day he would find his way.

She finally put her ears back on her head instead of having them glued to the garage door waiting for Darryl to come home. She gave up trying to think in his head. Brick by brick the wall came down.

The chaise was stopped in the classroom. It seemed like a good time to teach themselves new things about old truths. There was a royal awareness about being inside God's body. They were trying to be careful to observe and absorb All.

Imagine the speed at which thoughts operate in the natural. Step that speed up about eight quadrillions. Perhaps that will give you an idea about how fast things changed. In spite of the rapidity there was a spacious awareness that was comfortable, gentle and not in a hurry.

Beryle had her mind on spiritual growth and decided that she might have the hang of it.

She thought about the time when Emma invited her to be Women's Day Speaker at a rather large local church. Emma had planned four Saturday morning teaching sessions for certain women on the committees for the Women's Day. Those classes and the Sunday morning Women's Day event were successful. The people enjoyed the teachings and asked the Pastor to allow them to continue. The classes went for a semester and thirty five "Sprouts" graduated. They grew from a mobile Bible class to Spiritual Growth Ministries.

I Will Answer Before They Ask

When they entered the Realm of the Divine Spirit they could see what they believed, by faith. Their spiritual growth was a real journey through the "God Insides."

As they were making the journey they were not aware of all the things happening to them. They were changing effortlessly. The insides of God possessed them more and more completely. The object was to allow them to be conformed and consumed.

Complete union with God was the final destination.

God can happen to you.

Just because He is invisible to the naked eye does not mean He is not visible to the single eye. In Him is the Place to become transformed. When He made you, you came equipped with a God-shaped void and an urge to be re-united with Him.

The human desire to be united in marriage is a type – the two people can become one, only in flesh – because they are so dissimilar. Inside of God, the transformation will expose your spirit to the Translator who will gradually identify those dissimilarities and that which needs to be discarded. Throughout the journey the work of exposure operates at all times. As you take on, you put off. The images of strength, the images of steadfastness, and the idea of God parts might overwhelm you but you must keep going.

They moved effortlessly from the classroom back on to the chaise. As they slid along, on a flat chute, they discovered it was a long bone in God's right arm.

The Phoenix was perched near a gigantic light blue file cabinet. When Beryle saw it she wanted to pull a drawer out. The Phoenix flew right through the face of the third drawer and she could see inside. Her full name was on the tab that labeled the drawer. It began to expand and go on forever – like a long, long hall.

The whole thing was empty. Amazed that she knew why – she smiled all inside as she entered the file cabinet drawer. She could hear her own voice speaking about things that used to be in her future. No matter what she spoke the answer came, *"That is already taken care of for you."* She was speaking of what she wanted to see happen. In there, it had already happened. She was on the other side of the answer.

Drawer four was named for her too. It rose up into view – with no movement of the images. There, neatly stacked piles of DONE DEALS were filling themselves in individual slots and continuing at a fast pace – like information being down-loaded, flashing on a monitor. She asked a question. "God, what about the hard stuff and the messes I made?"

"Mess for whom? Whatever you deemed as hard stuff, I used as material to strengthen your root patterns. You like plants – you like to see things grow – so do I."

The Peace Place

The Peace Place in God was in His head. They had been afforded a tour through His trunk and down one arm.

They were reunited into one enormous mass of light and lifted off the chaise, as in floating, into the Peace Place.

Beryle was thinking, *In the natural, much that is important (and much that is not) goes on in the head. It takes serious application to connect head, heart, mind, will, spirit, ego, self, and emotions. How can I cause them to remain separate, yet make sense? Sometimes I get them mixed up when I try to categorize them. The need to do this is a self-check effort to be sure.*

I used to worry that "almost right is wrong." Now, since I am here in this Peace Place – that does not matter. I am thinking about how it feels to slide down into a bathtub filled with hot soapy water that makes friends with my skin – when tired muscles relax after I say a long ahhhh. For that brief time, until the unusual becomes usual – I do not care about "almost right is wrong." I could gather some idioms and ideas and bring them here and watch them melt.

There are definitions of peace, "the absence of war" is the first one to come to mind – I used to try to define it – when I saw it as an object.

Her thinking was interrupted. God said, *"Peace is a Place."*

One Monday night, while teaching the Bible class, Beryle was overcome with a need to settle some things in her life that were antagonistic to her and to some others. She decided not to say anything about them until she sorted them out and was living them.

With the plan flowing through the back of her mind, she continued teaching for a few sentences, then suddenly had the urge to sing, "I ain't gonna study war no more."

To her surprise and to all present, she sang and sang and sang and tears began to roll down her face. Her voice broke as she continued. Strangely, the class did not join her; some of the members began to cry. That went on for fifteen or sixteen clock minutes. It was as if the insides of her head were removed to make room for that new intention. There was no why connected – no wherefore – just "I ain't gonna study war no more."

She did not stop studying war that very night; she merely salted the ground to destroy the old growth that was in her heart to defend herself, establish her own rules about everything, and remain right forever. That crying event was an important milestone in her journey, much like a truck stop.

Her friend, Leon, owned an eighteen wheeler. It was held together with spit and spider webs. He bought it used. Sometimes she would run parts for him. He spent most of his at home time under the hood. She liked to ride with him on the short runs. The truck stops were interesting. There were large signs that said if you were not a trucker, do not sit at the counter – sit in a booth. Truckers got preferential treatment, faster service, much more food per serving and the unaccompanied drivers got smiled at a lot.

All the singing was an invitation to turn into God's Truck Stop. She needed to pull out of the busy traffic on her spiritual highway, to a place reserved just for her. There she could get a good meal, a cleansing shower and a bed in which to rest her weary bones. She did not know how tired she really was, until she took the offer to rest.

The cleansing cry washed away some of the crud of self-effort. It taught her she did not have to study war. There is no war in The Peace Place.

War issues continued– minor ones, no flags – no bugles – just things in places where there were issues. When she left the newly established Peace Place, she struggled. When she stayed there, yes was yes and her no was no and neither was coated with rationalization. That was a major breakthrough for Beryle. Her sister would tell her, "If they didn't already have rationalization, you would surely invent it."

You can approach God from the Peace Place. You get there by invitational revelation. You will know you are invited when you hear yourself say, "There must be a better way" or "There has to be more to God than this."

It was in the Peace Place that Beryle stopped listening for Darryl to raise the garage door when he finally came home. From there she learned to think forgiven instead being angry.

Their house could have gone from a wooded lot to a manicured lawn in four months; it took twenty-seven months. A mean-spirited, skinny housing inspector charged her with four hits for minor finishing touches that were left undone. He delayed their Certificate of Occupancy. Rather than to be angry with the mean-spirited inspector, she hung a spring-loaded fire door and corrected several building code deficiencies, herself. She could have drilled a hole right through the Hoover Dam with her determination. She had learned how to tape drywall and sand it during the construction. She also installed seventeen brass switch plates (minor little stuff). She did not try any of the hard stuff like digging holes for the 4x4's to support the deck.

George was in the late stages of renal failure which subsequently led to his demise. The experience of coming out of having gone through the building of their Murphy's Law house, dealing with dialysis appointments for George, being Pastor and teaching, actually forced her to need a Peace Place.

The Place of Practiced Stillness

When the overhead giant light set them back on the chaise, they went riding down God's right arm. A sudden stop jolted them. They felt a raw quiet, in a larger, more elegant classroom. The stillness there was what you feel when you hold your breath – a speared nothing. What if you threw a spear and it stopped in mid air?

The instructor was relaxed as in suspended flotation. She announced they were there to learn Practiced Stillness. Beryle's objectivity could not identify with that so she asked, "How do you learn a Place?"

She started to process her own question, *How many dimensions do you know? The need to express dimensions makes a Place, any one of which will merely define a space. Do you intend to capsulate a space? How much space is inside of you? How much of it is dedicated to noise, movement or activity? Go there and single out that which makes noise. Do you mean internal dialogue? Does it make noise? What would it take to quiet the noise? If you place your attention on it, will it act?*

God's answer came, *"It will do what it does. Where is the place of your inner activity? Let us presume that the busyness makes noise. In this Place there is a gravitational pull that calls you to suspension. You will not have to stay here past your ability to learn how to linger in the pull to permit it to ease you into the next Place."*

Every time you bump into God with the practice of stillness, you acquire a bit more of it. She used to wonder what it meant to *"BE STILL AND KNOW THAT I AM GOD."* (Ps.46:10a)

When Beryle was a little younger than four, her father would put a nickel near a footed Big Ben alarm clock on the mantle and say, "I will give you this nickel if you can be still and quiet for five minutes." She could not tell time. She would sit and listen to the ticking.

"Is it five minutes yet?" she would ask. Of course, you know she never got the nickel. Notwithstanding, was he teaching her the value of being still?

Their Grandpap Spires was a farmer in Southern Ohio – he owned a hundred acres. She and Dorothy spent summers there.

His routine brought him home about 3:30 in the afternoon. Their grandparents had a day bed with a padding filled with straw. It rested against an inside wall in their living room. Grand pap was 100 feet tall (to her). He had long skinny legs and a stiff-looking grey, handle bar mustache. He would sit and stretch his long legs out in front of him and rest his back against the wall, elbows on the bed with his fingers laced across his chest.

He would invite the little girls to sit there with him. Beryle remembered the first time she tried it. She was too short to stretch out like he did. Her best effort caused her to wiggle because her hands would not stay put.

"Grandpap, what are we doing?"

"Nothing."

She made it her business to be there every afternoon when he came in. He would come down around the side of the house and wash up with water from the rain barrel, using a small basin. He would throw the water over the side of the hill. After he ate his supper, he would tromp up the steps in his muddy, stiff brown tie-up high tops – to find her waiting to do nothing. He would tell her, "Shaggy, it's important to know how to do nothing." She would sit there for what seemed like two days and go to get up. He would stretch his long arm out to stop her, telling her, "Be still –you're learning how to do nothing. It's good for you. You will need it someday."

Ha! Was he God – the God of Psalm 46:10?

She was six years old wondering about God. (Not the scripture part)

That Place in God was not one of those endlessly large areas where roaming and looking were necessary. It was like a bus stop with seats under a glass shelter. Sit there long enough, a bus will come. She slid off the chaise and entertained a thought of the inside of God shrinking and becoming a bus stop.

Faster than her thought, an iridescent, slender, six-wheeled bus appeared. The six wheels allowed the bus to move sideways.

As the colors glistened, the bus seemed to breathe an invitation to board it.

She thought, *God must really be big inside – we have to ride a bus to get from here.* She laughed; *I have always wanted to drive a big bus so here is my chance.* As she climbed in the driver's seat, she noticed it was soft burgundy leather with white stitching. The bus began to fold around her. It took on her shape and she began to move. The image of the bus was gone. She was the bus.

"God, what happened to the bus?"

"You became the bus the moment you learned Practiced Stillness because it ushers you into the Place of Creativity. You become what you create and you can create whatever you like in this Place.

Practiced Stillness designs the vehicle that takes you to the Design Shop inside of Me."

"God, people do not want to know this, why?"

"They do, that is why they are reading this book. It is not that they want to know or do not want to know – they just do not remember. They have flashbacks of when they were in other places– just as you did.

"Do you *remember when you were trying to figure 'what world would there be if there were no world?' You thought of pain and decided it could not hurt to die because dying releases you from pain. You were five years old when you were thinking like that.*

"They told you I was doing My work when they heard thunder – you said, 'But what is God doing when it is not thundering?'

"They said you were 'fast'. Fast, at least. They spoke truth and did not know it. You were merely trying to associate fragments that had come unglued. You have made a gallant departure from those things they taught you – with resilient resistance.

"Everyone can create. Each one is part of the whole and creation is the whole. There is a rhythm to creation. It flows and recedes, ebb and tide – it is called Seasons".

"Can I move my bus backwards?" she asked.

"Of course you can. As long as you know you are moving it against the flow – (why would you want to) – you will drive it backwards to another Place and have to recoup the distance. In the Place of Creation there are no mistakes. That is why it is <u>one way</u> here."

The Place of Creation

The bus stopped.

It was about the zillionth time she wished she had six sets of eyes. That way she could look at everything at once. And she had (six sets). She was floating around like a bubble – turning and bobbing along – all eyes. She wondered how many things of one category she had seen at one time. She had seen a stadium filled with people, about 83,000. She had seen germs in a microscopic field doing business as teeming millions. That sight would not touch what she saw. And, it had cosmic order. Imagine seeing <u>all</u> the things from which dreams are made.

She wanted to gawk and strike herself with awe. Suddenly she knew. She had been there many times but just did not remember. Maybe she was never still enough to remember. But she was there then.

She remembered going to New York City – first time. There were twenty one models and several fashion designers, going to a fashion convention on a bus. All the while she was getting ready she kept telling herself – *stay with yourself. If you get to*

New York and the stuff whizzes by you, and you do not recognize that the time is whizzing by – New York City will be only a memory and you will not have enjoyed it. She called that living in the now.

She had all new pretty clothes, old shoes and three hundred dollars to spend (a handsome sum for her economic status). She tried to drink in the scenery. Summer on four turnpikes blurred against her expectations of the Big Apple. It did not disappoint her.

Their main event was a high-end fashion show at the Waldorf Astoria Hotel in the Starlight Roof Garden –where she had died and gone to heaven. While she was in New York she went to St. Patrick's Cathedral to give Darryl to God, which she found out later – did not come off too good.

Nancy Summers and she had walked down 5th Avenue where Beryle pretended to be posing for the famed ROTOGRAVURE. They stopped in a junky souvenir shop. She spent some of her money for a set of ivory and silver handled steak knives.

Back at their hotel that evening as she and Nancy walked into the lobby, a drop- dead gorgeous looking man, approached Beryle and asked her if she cared to dance. He was high maintenance for sure. His quiet demeanor matched his soft smile. She almost fell over herself as she extended her hand to say yes.

They went onto the dance floor and proceeded to create a "Some Enchanted Evening." He had a professional command of his dancing. He did not talk. He smiled a lot and just danced.

Over into the night the bar tender asked them to leave because the band was off the clock. He asked her if she needed a ride. She told him she was a guest in the hotel. He saw her to her room, said goodnight and the elevator ate him. She had not even asked his name. She beamed and swooned herself to sleep, too tired to think about her aching feet.

A week was long enough. The ride back home was the time to check to see if she had been careful to chew each delicious bite she had taken of the big Apple. She had! She did not miss a thing. She was aware of doing everything she had done. And she made it back home with no money, no regrets and the steak knives.

The bus started to talk to her. *"With effort and direction you can drive this bus along any street in Creation. Moreover, streets here are not crowded and there is no tailgating. Creativity is not peculiar to inventors and engineers. Everyone has it. Everyone can live in this Place. When this bus takes on your image and/ or you take on the image of the bus – you are what you create that creates you.*

"Sometimes caution is advisable because what you send out into Creation will come back someday and call you by your real name. Universal laws even things without any help from you. Creation is gravely interesting. Think about how the seasons change yet they are the same. The earth's heartbeat signals their movements.

"There are four changing seasons in some places, months of darkness in others – irreversible heat in the day that hides from the cold in the desert. These are signs and wonders that make

the substances of Creativity. This Place is everywhere you are. If you go to Practiced Stillness you will find the entrance to this Place – without fail. The substances exist. Lazy keeps creativity un-busy in most people."

She shook her head as she remembered the bus was talking. Their trip through the Places in God had not been as provocative as this one. It made her question what they were doing there. *What business would a person have inside of God? Perhaps to look around inside Him to see what makes Him HIM?* She was thinking – *what business do I have inside myself* – because *that is where the business comes from. The Main reason I do not go inside myself is that I do not really want to know what is in there for fear of pain. It might hurt to change. Deep inside, I might have to change me if I am going to let other people be who they are.*

Am I going to protect who I am by examining the importance of my ego and continue fighting to keep it? Maybe I am violating it. Did I grow from the last ego fight? Who won?

It occurred to her that she was having a "moment" in the Place of Creation. Deep in thought she felt like she was "becoming". Maybe she was fixing her ego with creative thinking. If not fixing at least working on it. Is that what creativity is?

The Place of Listening

The Phoenix was never far from them as they toured God's insides. They had no map and there was no itinerary for each destination. They were intrigued at how they arrived at various places and that one was no exception.

They changed from the bus image back into themselves at Creation Center.

There was an atmosphere of bustling excitement. It was a cross-town, mall-like area, exploding with shops, stands and display units. The billboard releases were moving messages advertising available Creativity items. Giant lettered words floated in the air telling of inventions and products waiting to be processed. They could see printed pages fanning themselves from books to be published. Current event releases were geared to those who were willing to be creative with them.

They walked with actual progress along a cloud like walkway, up to their knees in fluff. They stopped at an Ear shop. It was one giant ear carved out of a granite wall. The ear looked like a massive head in profile.

A hall vestibule arrangement directed them through a set of revolving bones shaped like the hammer, anvil and stirrup of the natural human ear. It was a little tricky passing through those revolving bones. They moved in a pulsing motion. Sound waves were causing the movement. It was exciting trying to get past them because they could not see where they were going. They had to hear their ways along and follow the sounds.

The fluff-like substance formed a bench. They sat down.

God is not complicated. If you want to know how to listen – go in His ear. The inner ear contains sensory perception for hearing and certain other receptors for equilibrium and the sense of position.

What they heard in God's ear was a systematic separation of weeping from crying, complaining from feeling sorry, *please don't God, don't let this happen, if you are God help me, don't help me, damn this, damn that, God said, God told me to tell you, God forgot me – If I do this, I'll ask for forgiveness later, there is no God, God who?*

There they were smack in the middle of God's ear watching the sensory receptors vibrate with the art of hearing. Her thought was that they were there to become sensory vibrators involved in the art of listening. If they were to do that, they would hear. That made her think about the times when she did not hear, even though she was trying to listen.

When Darryl was four, his father, who had divorced them, came to town and wanted to take Darryl to the movies. They were going to see Superman. Steve and Darryl came back; the report was that he cried all the way downtown, through the movie and refused the ice cream. He stood there pouting and exhausted. When he made eye contact with his mother, before she could ask him why he cried, he blurted, "Mommy, I told you I didn't want to go."

"God is listening an art?"

"No, it is a Place. When you come to the Place of Listening you will hear. When you came into My ear you heard what I hear – in your language. The wave distortion ruled out those languages you could not understand. You got the messages."

Before she could formulate the next question she knew the answer. *Pain producing egos teach pain avoidance.*

George needed some pain relief from a disc involvement in his back. He had prescriptions for pain pills. She had told him to take the pills close together so they would create a continuum in his body and combat the pain. He was afraid he would become addicted so he would wait until the pain was unbearable. He would suffer through the time it took the medicine to become therapeutic. He had occasion to go to a Pain Management Clinic where the doctor advised him to lace the pills every three hours around the clock and supplement with Ibuprofen. Soon he was comfortable. After he found relief, he told her, "I told the doctor you told me the same thing and I did not listen to you."

The advantage to listening is hearing with intent. You will know how better to act on what you hear, if you listen.

Beryle remembered her mother saying that sometimes the answer is in the question.

"Be sure to read the question." She had said. They were discussing an upcoming test in high school. That seemed strange to her teen-aged reasoning but she figured it out. Look in the question for the answer.

Listen for the indicators. The inner ear is past the noise vestibule. What will you hear?

Of notable interest is the fact that hearing is one way with no exit and no turnaround.

Hearing is what you do. The Place of Listening is where you go to hear.

The Place of Pure God

When they began their journey they were separate entities, recently unified by a common goal. They wanted to know God's insides. As they were invited to approach such a journey it became apparent that there was more theology than wisdom in what they had been taught in the traditional organized religious backgrounds from which some of them came.

They sat huddled in the Place of Listening enjoying each other's thoughts. They told stories of why they were not hearing because they were in the "first place" instead of the Place of Listening.

Suddenly, they heard a bell ring; not a doorbell, it was a school bell, not dongs but ring ring RING, two shorts, one long –it was clamorous. It broke the background waves and all sound.

From nowhere, several elongated tubes appeared and engulfed each of them. The tubes looked like transparent hot dogs. They began to move away from God's ear. They were lifted up in a gentle, smooth ride up, much like a modern elevator.

They saw stages and seats, vast fields of flowers, water in lakes and extended waterfalls. They could hear mighty rushing winds and a Still Small Voice, alternating inhalations of wind, exhaling the Small Voice. It was the same voice – coming in one way going out another.

They passed fire that looked like red and orange lava that made immense rock formations with great heat that did not consume the formations. They went up, up, and then grass.

The tubes stopped and they jumped out.

They began to run and play, frolicking like young children with garden hoses – spraying each other. There was no effort – no energy expense. They were neither winded nor tired. They just laughed and played with refreshing abandon. There was nothing to look at, no thoughts to think, and no questions – just freedom.

They made tree swings. One of them found five pretty little puppies happy to play.

It was Beryle's idea to look for horses. Soon as she thought about them, a stately, upper level dressage competitor trotted up to Beryle, she caught her breath. Everybody knew how she loves horses. She dared not try to ride it. Why not?? She found herself splitting the air in the saddle on that magnificent animal.

Valerie never had a bicycle as a child. She wanted one. Here was her chance to ride a bike. Soon as she thought about it, she remembered the bike ride in the famous movie ET. She found a little creature that resembled E.T.; put it in the basket on her bike and took off. She was screaming with excited laughter, waving back at them, Imagine, her first bike ride streaking through a vast nothing.

Rosa did not see her because she was busy making clouds. Her idea was to bounce on them. When she would try to bounce, they would expand sideways and cause her to roll over and over. She would try to catch onto the clouds to hold on for balance. That did not work. She just kept rolling, squealing with laughter.

Dorothy wanted to make bowling balls from one of Rosa's clouds. Because Rosa was rolling in them, Dorothy had to try to bowl and not hit Rosa. She decided to try to roll around Rosa. The cloud balls just took off and bounced up and down in circles, each returning to Dorothy's hand, to be sent out again. If was fun watching Dorothy as she tried to bowl. She was too tickled to catch the balls when they returned.

They played make-up and painted their faces. They did reflexology on Bonnie's feet. It began to rain. She gave new meaning to "foot loose and fancy free." The others laughed hysterically when she tried to sing "I got no strings to hold me down." She flopped up and down like a puppet who had become a real boy.

Sloshing around in the rain got them all muddy. They went plummeting straight down a hillside into a muddy pool that would not drown them. The muddy water splashed nicely.

The area was wooded. There were giant cedars, upside down trees, colossal redwoods, golden maple in white, green and gold resplendence. The taller ones reached up to forever. Scenery changed when they looked at them. The colors on the leaves changed in waves like the wind was telling them to move. They were not typical colors reflecting the season. The trees were alive with magenta, purple, and dynamic royal blue with super bursts of sparkle, like rapid fireworks.

"Let's do our nails– we could form a choir, let's grow some fruit – why not write a play about rock gardens and make the rocks into acrobats? Or, we could have a petting zoo?" They had settled down together, having a discussion when the Phoenix interrupted. They knew it was time to go from the Place of Pure God. They tried not to be sad.

Beryle thought the Place of Pure God would be all holy and spooky. The absence of the stained glass windows, choir robes and pews made her reflect and think. The dictates of clergy, the demands of the "thou shalt not's", and the dismay of inadequacy had fed the fear- of-God fire into her young life.

The Place of the Pure God was where she gave an erased closure to her other god – especially since he did not know her too well and never answered any of her "please-don't-let-this-happen" prayers. The evidence of that Place supported something she could embrace readily. Although she had always known God is ENERGY, she could not verbalize the concept because it played against the doctrinal charges that restricted her and her god.

Her god was limited by the knowledge of the persons to whom she spoke about him. When she asked what he was doing when there were no thunder and lightning, they told her to get somewhere and sit down. They taught her she should not question god and that in his own time and in his own slow way he would fix things – always after awhile. Early on, she knew she needed more information than they were giving her. An "after awhile" god did not seem to be good enough for her nor for the speed at which she needed to be moving.

At eight years old she discovered a small problem with god that might be fixed by joining the church. One Sunday she checked with Mildred Lawrence, also eight, and they joined the church together.

She was baptized in pomp and circumstance and ceremony. Her mother cried, the water was almost hot, her hair got wet and the preacher held her nose. It was appropriately Easter. Beryle had hoped she would feel new. Surely, Easter could accomplish that especially with the resurrection and all. All she felt was wet and the same, but that did not stop her.

She made a major vow to be good as she could and to stop lying, now that she was a real Christian.

Being good was easy. In order to extract the lying out of her, she soaked in the tub the next Saturday night and prayed real hard to be able to stop lying. That is what her mother called it, she would say, "You'll tell a lie to see if one will come out of your mouth."

Beryle did not see it as lying. They were stories to test the grownups who should have known not to believe the tales. Her neighbors were delighted with the little girl's entertaining antics. The remarkable thing was they did believe her. When she decided to stop making up stories, she had to recant and say the stories were not real – "But what I am saying now is real."

A mess! Yes! She had to re-think the god business because if god were all that then why did he let her get into all this. No doubt having that energetic, open, eager little person in the home was taxing and trying to her mother. Beryle pushed and pulled through the years with a bullhorn in one hand and an ink pen in the other.

At seventeen, she set about to find truth. It was apparent to her that their kindly old Pastor did not have answers to her questions. The God-will-take-care-of-you syndrome did not quite square with why the boys did not like her. Waiting for god to fix that was a jail sentence. She figured she could move on to acting or discovering the real truth while she waited for god to fix stuff.

Some years later that idea took her to Metaphysics lectures, free every Tuesday night. She announced that she had come to find truth. Nobody was impressed. Soon she learned to sit in the silence, center herself, release tensions and concentrate.

Instead of the proverbial truth for which she was looking, she found herself. She had never put the two together. Was she truth? One of the major reasons she had for looking for truth was that she had a problem with her feelings being hurt all the time. She had been there several months before she asked the master, "How can I rise above personal injury to my feelings?"

He sat very still and lowered his head. He was a slim, white haired, lovely person with a voice that was almost audible. After what seemed like forever, he whispered, "Whenever your feelings are hurt, you are wrong."

Well, that was the end of that. He had hurt her feelings. She was ready to bop out of there and go somewhere else to find truth. On the way home, Lula, friend and neighbor said, "Why not think about what he said? It makes sense to me."

It made sense to Beryle, too, but she was so used to defending herself from all quarters, it was hard for her to buy his diagnosis. She discovered it was her decision to be or not be hurt, offended, put upon and/or insulted. Life became easier and she continued in the lectures for twelve years.

She learned some powerful truths the following years. The god of the army of "Onward Christian Soldiers" was discharged. The war was over for Beryle. She walked away from her programmed commission in his army.

The complicated god of our fathers faded into a simple idea that <u>God is</u>. That was it. That was what she found after everything, everywhere. She was looking for who they said He was and found <u>I Am</u> – who is who He said He is. That is pure God.

The Place of God's Heart

When the group was ushered from the Place of Pure God they were lined up single file walking on thin red strings. There was one for each foot. It surprised her that she did not have to balance. They looked like embroidery thread. The strings were not attached to anything, nor were they far out in front of them. They were extended as needed. No slipping, no almost, no need to balance even though they were suspended across emptiness. The emptiness was not dark or black, it was just empty. Since there were no landmarks they did not know in which direction they were headed.

A Major Angel appeared. She was not sure if he were major by rank or major by importance, as opposed to minor or both. She knew who he was and she knew each of them saw a different image though there was only one Angel.

She greeted him by thought. *I know you. You are the one who helped me when I needed to jump from a second story balcony because the Best Western Motel was on fire!*

Beryle was part of a medical research team called S.E.N.I.C. It was a government funded study to determine why patients got certain infections after a hospital stay, when there were no infections upon admission. They traveled in teams across the USA to hospitals doing what was called a Retrospective Chart Review. They had been trained in Atlanta, Georgia at the Center for Disease Control. They were Medical Record Technicians. Her ten member team left Plantation, Florida assigned to a hospital in Indianapolis, Indiana. They drove cars and vans issued by the Government.

The motel was brand new. They checked in, unpacked and had free time. It was early evening. The leaders went to find the hospital; some went to find grocery stores. Beryle and two others went to Braille the facility. She wanted to see how the motel was designed. The team had been in four other motels and never had done that.

The place was shaped like a horseshoe with rooms in the round part of the horseshoe. The office, kitchen and dining room were in what would be the open space of a horseshoe – as if joining the two ends across.

The three of them found a sauna in the basement of the two-story motel; they put on bathing suits and sat. Because she was so tired from the long drive, it seemed a good thing to do. Soon she was uncomfortable there; not from the heat. There was an old familiar unhappy feeling of not liking to be shut up in close places, especially in a basement. She left them.

For a while she dinged around in her room and decided to sleep. They had been on the road for many hours; most of them were spent getting across Texas. Later, that evening, the "kids" were going across the road to dance at the Holiday Inn. They asked her if she wanted to join them. (She was much older than they) She told them no and dozed off with the television on.

In her sleep she heard awful acid rock music – and woke up to find a rock group slicking at her eardrums. There was a banging on the door which, she decided, was the kids – wanting to tell her about all the beer and the guys... she had been in a deep sleep.

She got up to turn off the television, ignored the banging on the door and took a look out the sliding glass door and WHAM, she woke up!

The entire area of the office, kitchen and dining room was one mass of white. She could see steel girders bending over like they were melting with heavy tops. FIRE!

She began to talk to herself. *"Beryle, think! This place is on fire. That banging on the door was a warning to wake up. What do you know about fires? Don't open the door. Touch the door to see if it is hot. Think! Don't panic! Look outside! You could die if you do something wrong here. Put your clothes on. Put on pantyhose, underwear, a sweater and you coat – better put on some slacks* (it was late April). *Get your car keys. Get your identification. Think! Go out on the balcony. Close the sliding glass door."* She did all of that.

Out onto the balcony she noticed there was no one in the courtyard. Her room faced the inside of the horseshoe. There was another room on the opposite side, across the hall behind her room that faced the parking lot.

When they had brailed the building, she found there were doors that allowed access to an inner courtyard at four points around the horseshoe, each leading to the surrounding parking lot.

If you were to walk through one of the doors on the round part of the horseshoe, straight from the parking lot, you would pass the length of one room, cross a corridor, pass the length of an opposite room, then enter the courtyard through an interior door. A small kidney shaped swimming pool with water in it, was surrounded by grass. It took up less than half of the court yard. Some of the space had small wrought iron tables and chairs. Balconies and porches allowed guests to enjoy being out of doors in limited privacy.

The spanking brand new motel was involved in a serious five alarm fire. When she stepped onto her balcony, there was no one in sight. She was on the second floor – she yelled a plaintive "HELP!" Then she thought, *Don't do that!! If you get your lungs full of smoke you could die – don't yell. Besides, there is no one to hear you and who could help you if he did hear you?* She looked down. There was cement under her balcony. There was grass under the balcony next door to the right. The balconies were separated by a wrought iron railing. She knew she was going to have to jump. She decided to cross over the railing – careful not to burn herself – the railing was hot.

She could hear fire sirens in the far distance. Her plan was to get into the swimming pool and wait for the rescuers. She got over the railing, with a major imitation high jump and checked to see if the grass were still there. That was when she saw HIM, the Major Angel.

He had on a short sleeve shirt with blue thumbprints on a white background. The prints were three different shades of blue. The sight of him startled her. She froze.

Across the courtyard, a man in his pajama bottom took an abandoned leap over the railing from his balcony on the second floor. The thud sounded and lingered. Then a half naked female with a hat on appeared. She came from the same room onto the balcony. Perhaps she was going to jump, too. The second she saw his freeze frame, face down on the ground, she began screaming. Beryle was staring thinking, *I wonder if she is going to jump, too?*

Her plan was to hang and drop. She learned that from her fire fighter friend, John. When they spent time together he talked about survival during a fire. Black smoke was creeping away from the white part of the burning structure which was a golden red a minute or so later.

The man with the thumbprint shirt yelled up at her, "Jump!" That brought her back to the moment. She looked down at him. Then he hollered, "Jump!" louder and more forcefully. Over the rail and down she jumped. He reached for her to break her fall. She landed hard, standing straight with purse, car keys, trench coat and all.

He wrapped his arms around her holding her close to him. Her shivering body was trying to collapse. With a gentle push, he whispered, "Go that way all the way to the end and wait there for me." He was pointing to what was the round part of the horseshoe.

She ran to the end of the courtyard away from the creeping fire smoke and stood shaking. She could not stop shaking. Her breath was coming in spurts almost with every other shake. Soon her attention was drawn to the faces on people gathered there. One small lady with red stringy hair was crying into her rosary beads. Everyone was standing in a huddle, captured by morbid fear.

A middle aged man with a briefcase appeared on the balcony, from his room, on the ground floor. He was fully dressed; suit and tie. He leaned backwards, holding on to the rail with his left hand. He took deliberate aim, and was able to sling his briefcase over his head onto the balcony above. Then he climbed on the rail to his room and jumped himself up to the floor above him and climbed up to that balcony, over the rail. She was stunned with unbelief as she watched him pick up his briefcase and lean backwards again, over the railing and sling the case up onto the roof. How he managed to climb up onto that roof will probably remain a secret in the Annals of the American Journal of Adrenaline. The last time Beryle saw him he had his briefcase and was standing on the roof.

The man with the thumbprint shirt appeared. He did not look tired nor was he dirty. He was politely calm as he said, "If I go through that door," pointing to one of the four doors that led to the parking lot, "Where will it lead me?"

She barely whispered, "To the parking lot."

She had forgotten him. Her attention was focused on trying to figure out how the briefcase man managed to climb onto the roof...adrenal fear. That was it. She was thinking about that when the man in the shirt, with the thumbprints, took her arm and led her nearer to one of the doors that led to the parking lot.

"Stand here until I come back." he said, still calm, and still a little above a whisper. He disappeared through the door.

There was no area light as provided by the motel. By that time the electricity had been compromised. They were able to see because the fire lit the night. The atmosphere was not yet filled with smoke, but soon would be. She could see the smoke playing between grey and black in giant rolls. The wind was blowing.

One of the team members came up to Beryle and said, "Did you have any trouble getting here?" she gestured to the area around the door. That question brought her attention back from the smoke.

Beryle opened her mouth to say no and "Jesus" came out. They were both surprised. The surprised girl backed away.

The man in the shirt appeared again. Holding the door open, he said, "Beryle, I am going to push you. Take a deep breath and run fast as you can in a straight line. You will come to an open door. You will be safe.

Breathe!! Run!!" He pushed so hard that she would have fallen down had she not known he was going to push. She ran hard; fast. Through the door was pitch black soot smoke. She knew where she was going because they had "Brailed" the fancy new motel.

Wham! She slammed into a mass! It was not an open door. Going fast, she wanted to knock it down whatever it was. It was a policeman. He grabbed her with both arms, lifted her and whirled her around. He held her so close that she could feel heat from his badge against her body. He turned her around two times and put her down.

Still holding her close to him he said, "You're safe, you're safe now!" He wanted to make sure she had her footing before he let her go.

What should she do now? She did not know if she should relax or cry or say thank you or what. He let her go. She was coughing and crying and scared and shaking, trying not to vomit. She just stood there because she was safe.

The policeman said, "Go that way and keep going until you get to a chain link fence and you'll be safer there." He pointed in the direction that would lead her to the highway. She started to walk and decided to run and then walk. Maybe the chain link fence would be near. When she got to the chain link fence, she realized she was really safe. She came back to her original self.

The team members showed up. They were hugging and counting each other.

A nervous, excited man approached them and announced himself as the Manager of the Holiday Inn across the road. He said if they were registered at the Best Western, they could go across the highway and get free accommodations.

Cynthia and she walked together across the road into the unoccupied lobby. It was 3:36 a.m. The night clerk came from behind a wall and gave each of them a registration card. They had not said much to each other.

As they were writing on the cards, the man in the shirt with the blue thumbprints said, "Beryle, are you alright?" He was at her left side.

She looked at him and said, "Yes."

"Are you sure?"

"I'm sure." she answered just above a whisper as she turned her attention back to the card.

Cynthia said, "Who are you talking to?"

"Don't you see that man standing there?" Beryle made a gesture, as a matter of fact.

"What man? You must be in shock."

They learned later that the man with the briefcase broke both his legs when he jumped from the roof. The side of the building that faced the parking lot had no balconies. The man who jumped over the railing died. Roma, one of the team members, died. She was with Beryle in the sauna. She ran out from her room into the hallway that was filled with black smoke.

They were walking on the red strings, when Beryle saw the image of the Major Angel. She had a flashback of the fire because he was the man in the shirt with the blue thumbprints. She remembered he had called her by her name. Can angels wink? She thought she saw him wink at her.

When Beryle was preparing to go to Africa she was praying about the plane ride. She remembered having seen this very same angel image. He had one foot in America and one foot in Africa, with a teeny little airplane on his right hand. He bent

84

over and lowered his hand at a decline to allow the little airplane to roll off his middle finger in Lagos, Nigeria.

When Kelley, Darryl's son, was in the third grade, some bigger boys were bullying him at school. His granddaddy wanted to go to school to take care of those boys. His grandmother prayed. As she was praying, she saw images of two enormous angels escorting Kelley to school.

They appeared to be about eighteen feet tall. One was behind him, the other one was alongside him. They were enormous and he looked teeny tiny little. They waited for him to take six or eight steps before they even shifted their weight to move. He was lumbering; they were hardly moving. Angel images were not strange to Beryle and she never questioned their appearances; or their existence.

Thoughts were flashing as she walked along on the extended strings. She was enjoying the unique sweetness of being inside of God. Was that the Place where God's heart strings were wound up on a roll? Does it have a gravitational pull?

The Place of New Higherness

They were walking softly because the strings looked so delicate. There was no balancing. It was like everyday walking. There was no need for a safety factor, even though they were suspended in raw nothingness. Everywhere in God is safe. In spite of the perfectly outrageous things they had seen, they never sensed they were unwelcome.

When Beryle was in London, England, with the models, their tour went to Buckingham Palace. Aside from hoping everyone she knew, in the whole round world, would somehow find out she was there, she was hoping to see everything in that famous palace. Awestruck and wide-eyed she was taking mental pictures of every detail along the guided tour. She was so caught up in her sightseeing (because they did not permit cameras) somehow she managed to wander off away from the tour.

One of the palace guards walked up behind her, and in his royal Brit accent, suggested she might join her tour "through this door – this way out." She found herself in a dirty old alley. Of course, she would not want her friends to know she had been ushered out of Buckingham. It would be enough for them to know she was there.

That stood in contrast to the comfortable ease in which they moved along inside God from the Place of God's Heart. They were on their own. Beryle could not see the bird or the Major Angel – in fact, she did not see the others. That tried to become scary so she breathed, in and out; profoundly aware of being inside of God.

She was wondering: Who are you – really? Not to God, but to yourself. How would it feel being Beryle, on the inside, looking at an X-ray machine –looking out from the inside? If that part were aware of having its picture taken, how would it feel? Perhaps it would wonder why. Maybe it would notice something that needed to be fixed and the picture might help. It occurred to her that she might be naked and decided it did not matter. They had been enveloped in light all along and they had each other and were comfortable because they were such good friends.

Bonnie would sit at the table in the class and take notes. Sometimes she had a question or a comment. She was soft spoken and prone to deep, generous laughter. Frequently, she added dimension to the subject matter that bounced around the table. The proverbial light would come on in her sharp understanding, she would lay her pen down, close her book and whisper, and "We can go home now."

Dorothy came to the class because Danna, their hostess' daughter, insisted. They worked together in Pediatric Specialties at a major hospital. Dorothy resisted; Danna insisted. Dorothy gave in and bowled out at one league game and came to the class. It was winter about fourteen degrees. She sat through the class. When it was over she and the teacher left together. Dorothy wanted to confide in the teacher. What followed was a sad, sorry story of boy meets girl and girl and girl and boy treats original girl with indifference in return for soap-opera devotion. The answer was, "You do not have to live like that. We can show you a more excellent way. We can teach you how to change your mind"

The bowling league was put on her back burner. She came faithfully to the Thursday Night Bible Class.

Rosa came to a program Beryle was teaching in the mid-eighties called Victory Over Weight. It was a Scripture based approach to the fact that people overeat because something is eating them.

Rosa was fascinated with the program almost as much as she was fascinated with the teacher. Rosa told Beryle, one day, "I am not going to church anymore until you open one."

"What if I don't?"

"Then I won't go, but you will."

Rosa had been with Spiritual Growth Ministries several years before they started the Thursday night class. In one class the students were asked to tell of something they could do, that would earn money for them. Rosa said she could bake rolls. She brought samples to the class. That was the birth of Heaven Scent Rolls, which made a way for her to quit her good job where she was a highly paid social worker. She founded a profitable business.

Valerie found her way to the Thursday class at the invitation of the hostess' other daughter, Marie. They were in a Sunday school class together.

Val held a position with a Property Management Group for which she had written a proposal, for $4.6 million from the U.S. Government, to renovate the properties. That was during a time when nobody was getting money from the Appropriations Committee. Val said the people in the office, the ones who wanted the money, did not expect it. Using principles she learned in the Bible class, she spoke of the money, at all times, as though they already had it. It was a Tuesday when the call came from Washington that the money had been appropriated.

Surely, the same God who moves mountains and guides eagles through pathless air can orchestrate appropriations. That was her story to those worry- wart unbelievers in her office. The other place, less than Higherness, is where people worry and shut down. Worry shuts down the hearing. It is hard to hear from God and worry at the same time.

The Phoenix was gone. The Major Angel was not there and the light was gone, too.

Again, Beryle wondered if she were naked. What if she were naked before God? That could be embarrassing. Whew!

She remembered she was naked IN God. That threw a different light her way. *If I am in Him then I cannot see me – I see only Him. If He sees me, He will look right through me. That would be just like God looking in a mirror.* That thought slipped out and surprised her.

"Be still and know that I am God."

She tried to turn off her thinking mechanism in an effort to be still. And the thoughts rolled on. Actually, she did not know how to be still. Hearing it from God presented a concern. She could not think how to do both at the same time. She decided just to "be". She wanted to reduce her outer and allow her inner to grow. Perhaps that would help.

Then, a calamitous thing happened!!

A mysterious looking box jumped up in front of her. That jerked her to her senses. She heard a deafening, loud box noise. The gigantic box was dark brown like coffee grounds. There were fuzzy slats that defined its shape. The spaces between the slats began to vibrate and shake. The noise was sustained and became the sound of a deep" Om". (the meditative chant sound) It surprised her because there was a stillness lesson going on.

Mesmerized, she watched the strange box move and sound as it expanded in four different directions. It stretched and moved until the outside of it was so big she could no longer see dimensions. It reminded her of how a life raft expands.

Music filled the area inside the box. It sounded like a full blown classical orchestra at a dynamic mezzo forte. All the music sounded like one major harmonious "Om". Perhaps that is what smoke sounds like to the wind. The music softened and took on images of multi- colored music notes. There were millions. They flew around like birds; tiny little fat and skinny creatures swaying as if riding on wind currents the" Om "sound made. They began to circle with a gentle wave; they moved her and floated her inside the gargantuan box.

It was a theater.

She just stood there in explicit wonder. She saw tiered balconies filled with people. The occupants were each and every person she had ever seen or had seen her, living or dead. Imagine there being a ticket for every single encounter by sight or touch, or by those merely passing and having caught a glimpse of her. A ticket bought for those barely brought into focus, yet aware of her.

He said, *"These are your fields of possibilities. You touched them with your spirit in the Universe. That is what attracted any one of them to interact with you in your never ending play. That is the IS, WAS AND EVERMORE SHALL BE production you are working on now. Coming inside of Me gave you opportunity to block the next few scenes. You might say you are having a Notice of Audition call. Those on the front rows are waiting to read your script. You selected them and you are now blocking the scenes before they try out. That action goes on in your thought processes as you produce, direct and act your own play.*

Here, inside Me you can become familiar with the end and the beginning. I will always cause you to know the end first. That is why you came.

This is a pre- opening run through, to iron out the kinks and to set the timing of the production. The production is for the subscribers and for the sponsors – All of you.

Perhaps you have never thought of Me being in the audience watching your production. It might surprise you to know I am neither critic nor reviewing media. I am a paying subscriber, there to enjoy the show. Inside eternity, there is never an ending, thus the play goes on until you decide to close it down, at which time you set about to write another.

Somehow, she knew she WAS the theatre of her life. All the plays in her theatre were who she was!!!

An animated excitement caused her to shiver. She did not know if she were seated or standing. Things began to appear and turn into scenes.

Is there a difference between looking and watching? And all of this is going on inside of God? She was thinking, again.

A play was being mounted in the spectacular new theatre with all new seating, an orchestra pit, lights, stage and a house. She saw a panoramic review of her history. The scenes depicted things she had experienced, and did not know how or why beforehand.

As the events were reviewed she realized she was seeing the workings of the INVISIBLE; the behind the earth-life arena of her life. It was a depiction of the God-work on her behalf to affect the mechanics of the choices she had made and was going to make. There were bits that included the Major Angel image running interference to correct those things that would shift and cause different results.

The theatre was filled with faces of people she knew from childhood and even then. She saw the lady from the neighborhood gas station store that was kind to her one morning. She left there and made up the idea of passing out Kindness Certificates from the church – with ten-dollar bills in the envelopes. The kindly little lady smiled and nodded at her. Beryle never told the lady about them. She was glad to see the lady and glad she knew about the certificates even though she never got one. She was able to recognize some people a few rows back.

Her deceased father-in-law waved a program at her. His broad grin was so familiar. He was the one who helped her learn the rules for driving. He taught her to pull her car out under the light when turning left, whenever possible, to "allow the other fellow a chance to turn, too."

Rows and rows were filled. In the front rows were people she was yet to meet. The strange, the covenant breakers and self-righteous people who would not like her were there, too. Each of them had a penny to contribute to the cost of her experiences to come.

She did not know if she were the star of the event or an innocent bystander. Somehow, she did know she was the playwright – to cast and plot the "WAS, IS NOW AND EVER MORE SHALL BE" of her life, notwithstanding, the unchangeable past.

When Beryle looked at the audience some of the people stood up and began to change places with each other, hurrying to be in the next scene. They would come up onto the stage to be in her future. They waited in the wings backstage.

Waves of colors began to flood the house as the forever orchestra tuned.

A gigantic curtain appeared and enclosed the stage. The baton tapped on the music stand in the orchestra pit. The orchestra developed an immediate attentive silence. The curtain opened and she could see the props for her future in organized perfection. Music whispered loveable wind songs in wake-up trios. Energetic lilts went out from the invisible orchestra, charming music with magic harmony, graceful, yet strong.

Characters from stage right and stage left appeared, waiting for validation from her. When she looked at them they were immediate animation. When she looked away dissolved into the atmosphere.

The disappearing people made her to know why they came here. That was why anyone would want to be inside of *God – to see the future.*

It was ultra clear to her that God did not make, nor did He hold her future.

She had the impulse to belt out a few phrases of Over the Rainbow. She was on stage. Soon as the impulse became apparent, her contralto voice began to thunder. The music changed to accompany her. Surprised, she stopped; it stopped. She began thinking again.

Where is this place?

Is it at the end of the two red strings?

What is this theatre called?

"NOW, is the name of this Place. It is the essence of your is-ness", God said.

After what seemed a few minutes or all day, Beryle wanted to review what she had heard: a Place called Now. She tried to talk to herself, inside. *I am the "I Am" and whatever play I can conceive is to be mounted on this stage in God's heart.*

He merely backs the production by providing the stage, props, stagehands, costumes, etc. He even arranges for the promotion and public relations, moreover; He provides the audience.

Or, I can do that. I can stay here in His Heart and learn to produce what I write. I can write the play. This is the Place where the play happens before it is written. It is acted out in the Heart of God then presented to the public. You might say this is the off-Broadway run. This is where it is tightened up before it goes to New York.

And God said, *"AMEN"*

Wrapped in the Power

The others were in their own theatres blocking and rehearsing their own lives. Just think, what if you could set your life up the way you really wanted it before it is presented to the world – just like a play? *Good question*, she thought.

There were two gigantic sliding glass doors on the back side of the stage. All her life's future characters were waiting in the audience backstage. The rest of the world was out there through the enormous glass doors.

She had begun to think again. *How can I pull this off? How can I fix my play and have it presentable for those out there? I wonder if authors write with a silent concern for those who will read their stuff. (Even as I write this, I am conscious of you reading it. It is as if you are here now listening to me think this – and for sure you are, because you are in my play. You are one of my characters even as I am in your play – at this very moment.)*

As she thought about her life's play, the Phoenix appeared, fluttering excitedly. They followed it into a Costume Place.

Wow!! It was like the inside of a majestic hotel with interior balconies and sky lights that could be seen from the main floor. There were elevators, mirrored in gold. The shining railings had elaborate plant material hanging in floatation from them. Gracious cerulean colors were whisking in and out among the varied leaves and flowers. The plant material did not move – the colors did – like playful butterflies pulling bands of ribbons that turned into clouds when they touched the leaves and flowers.

That movement should be made into music. When she thought that, a carillon sounded like delicate crystal wind chimes. They were the sounds daffodils make when they smile. She heard the whisper of a blooming orchid; mingled with songs of morning doves.

Along the railed corridors of the vast atrium were shops for the Costumes of Life. Beryle lifted her thoughts to propel herself onto level sixty, aware of, but not concerned with her nakedness. She wanted to select a garment or two, perhaps an outfit.

She went into an expanse that had no doors – there were no clothes –just ideas. To finger ideas was quite a challenge. Each one was different. She planned to put them together to make outfits – why not make a wardrobe? That was a Place she could imagine; a Place where ideas were just hanging around.

In June, when Beryle turned five she wanted to go to school. She could not go until September. Dorothy had been going for two years. She would teach Beryle what she learned. That was good, but Beryle wanted to be the teacher and Dorothy would have no part of it.

She would say, "You can't be the teacher, you have not been to school yet."

Beryle's thought was if she had been taught, then Dorothy should be the student and let Beryle be the teacher. Then Dorothy could see how good a teacher she was because her little sister had learned what she was taught. That did not fly either.

Evon and Jenny lived across the alley. Evon was Dorothy's age and they were inseparable in school. When they were home they would spend time together and would not include Beryle and Jenny, who was three. Jenny, then, was the likely candidate for home schooling in Miss Beryle's class. When she was made to sit still on the steps of the front porch, her attention span would tell her to cry and want to go home. That was plan A.

Beryle had a small business those days. She would walk the neighbors' dogs for free. Her father had given her a roll of rope – the kind he used to hang windows. He had cut the rope into pieces for her. She tied them to the porch railing. The idea for walking the dogs was to bring them home and tie them to the porch to teach them what Dorothy had taught her. They had school every day that she could manage it. Some days she would be able to teach Jenny and the dogs. Her mother would let her play in the rain. On rainy days school went on just the same. The little teacher would put the dogs under the porch and teach them through the lattice. That was plan B.

Far back as she could remember she wanted to be a teacher. She would organize a parade. Each child would have a noisemaker. Usually, it was one of her mother's roasting pans or pots that she could manage to sneak out of the house. They were to hit the pans with sticks to make the marching noise. She did not call them drums. They were musical instruments. She learned that from Dorothy. Even the parade was a form of school. She would be the teacher. She would trick them into being students via the parade.

Her father knew. She was his "kitten". He would put her on his knee and they would form a flock of geese. They would become part of the flock and would fly away over the Blue Ridge Mountains or out over Nova Scotia to see all the places they wanted to go. They would not have to ride the train, nor buy tickets, because they could fly.

There were places he knew in his heart. He taught her a song called *Let the Rest of the World Go By* (Brennan & Ball):

> *With someone like you*
> *A pal so good and true*
> *I'd like to leave it all behind and go and find*
> *A place that's known to God alone*
> *Just a spot to call our own*
> *We'll find perfect peace where joys never cease*
> *Out there beneath the kindly sky*
> *We'll build a swell little nest*
> *Somewhere in the West*
> *And let the rest of the world go by.*

He was a dreamer. She adored him.

"Daddy, where do houses come from?"

She remembered him laughing as he told her, "They grow. You just plant a chair and a davenport and some dishes and wait a while and your house will grow. The more furniture you plant, the bigger the house."

That called for a project for her five-year-old scientific mind. She got a sand shovel and an old tablespoon and began to dig along side of the house. It took a few days for her to dig her secret hole deep as her little arm could reach. She knew how to put water in the hole to make mud so it would be easier. Since the house was deep as she could dig, it must be true. She knew some of the stuff was her father's geese flying stuff – but that was real.

Her idea of wanting to be where they had ideas is not new. She had some. Some she used and some used her. In that Place there were gazillions of ideas, all suspended from high wires made of orange colored yarn. She was wide eyed almost breathless with excited anticipation. As she fingered the wearable ideas, they seemed soft. When they identified themselves as: Belligerence, Domination, Martyrdom, Silliness, Anxiety attacks, Shunting, Gossip, Laziness, and Procrastination, she decided to stop touching them. When she did they took on the form of a conveyor line, like in a dry cleaning place. As they began to move before her each one was clearly identified. It was like being in a dictionary factory, idea after idea. It occurred to her that they were changing in degrees of seriousness. She wondered about them because it seemed they were so harsh. As they progressed the lovelier ideas came into view: graciousness, allowing, respectfulness, dependability, softness, and gladness.

Perhaps they represented qualitative increases with spiritual growth. The dynamics levels of the ideas increased beyond her understanding.

She calmed down and toyed with the idea of a label for her God garment. What would God's label look like? Would it have a green stitch somewhere to authenticate it? If so, certainly it could not be duplicated. That eliminated the label, besides who would care?

Her attention was drawn back to the fanning ideas. It was like trying to pick from thousands of coats. She reached and touched one. The revolving stopped.

The idea she touched began to move. It was her size, in an iridescent chiffon-like substance; it was not fabric though it looked like fabric. It was not a dress, it was a poncho. Poncho sounds too harsh for it. It was like a poncho. There was no hanger, it just appeared. When it did all the other ideas kept moving.

She put her arms up expecting the item to float down over her head. It began to whirl and dance above her, which created a vacuum that scooped her up into it. She was assimilated. She was consumed. No energy, no pressure, no temperature, She disappeared. She became the garment.

"You are the POWER of Love. You are welcome everywhere you are; you are everywhere. You can wear it, use it, give it away, sit on it, bathe in it – it is all purpose...by the way, it has a label: ONE SIZE FITS ALL."

The Kingdom of God

The others were experiencing the Places in God along with Beryle. She did not need to check with them because she knew they were having the same experience.

That Place, inside of God, inside of the Theatre of All Potential, in the Costume Atrium must have been near to the third heaven. Was that the third heaven? Ha. There is a thought, *Is heaven inside of God?*

There was a soft sense of completion that suggested the end was near, except she did not want it to be over. Her thoughts of movement ushered her through an opening near the tall tree standing on a footed base. The tree bowed and swayed when she looked at it. She was in a Place that had 360° of mirrors. No matter which way she looked she saw herself. Each image was different. Some she liked.

There was the tattletale little girl who wanted to be right all the time. She saw the tearful teenager clinging to her divorced father.

She saw herself, in a drama class, elated because she had threaded an imaginary needle. It was a pantomime requirement for which the teacher made a public compliment.

In senior high school the uncomfortable majorette uniform itched. She had to march on a muddy football field during an away game. The mud sucked at the boots she tried desperately to keep on her feet. The principal of that high school sent a letter to her school to ban her from marching there ever again because she was "suggestive."

As the mirror images continued, she was almost undone. *All of that is almost impossible for one person to have survived. You might want to complement yourself.* That thought was almost playful.

When she saw one particular image, she remembered the embarrassment. In the high school senior play, she had to play a few measures of Beethoven's Fifth Symphony on the piano, slam the cover down, get up and walk away.

When she did that, the cover flipped off the piano and hit the stool. When she pushed back trying to get up, she and the bench fell over. At that point the audience thought that was supposed to happen – until her father stood up in the balcony and yelled, "Oh my God, now I have to buy a piano."

She saw an excited, scared young girl on the train with at least two hundred other students going and returning to colleges. Her mother had tucked a small piece of folded tablet paper in Beryle's pocket and said, "Read this when you get time." It was six or seven weeks before the new freshman found time to read it. In pencil her mother had copied the words to a hymn by Robert Thompson entitled *I Would be True* (for there are those who trust me).

Those refreshed incidents seemed so very present, yet too far away. She watched herself for a while. She swallowed hard trying not to cry.

The mirrors continued to reflect the things that had shaped her through life and not without a somber, sweet pleasure. She laughed and sighed and clapped her hands. She covered her face, wiped tears, as she watched her very life in the Mirrored Hall. If she had stayed there she would have been there still.

The Phoenix appeared with a small card in its mouth which it sent toward Beryle by lifting its head. As the card approached, she saw a cord attached to it which settled around her neck. It was an identification card. She was to have a picture made to go on the card. She smiled; a light flashed. When she picked up the card there was a hologram on it with at least three hundred and sixty five faces. Each one was a pixel to form the whole face.

The I.D. card had no writing. When she looked at it the faces came to life to depict the attitude of each image. They caused the picture to look as if it were breathing. It was soft and dimensional. Every expression was distinctive.

Is this the way God sees me? Do I look like a hologram? She thought, as she allowed the I.D. card to rest on her chest.

What about her feet? She had no shoes. She had been concerned about her nakedness. It was covered (pun intended). Her God garment made her think about an outfit. She had no shoes. In the Mirrored Hall she did not want to go any further without shoes. Wondering about the shoes, she heard noises. They were thoughts clinking around as if bumping into each other. It was the group. They had their hologram tags around their necks, too. They were looking at their feet. Obviously, they had experienced the Mirrored Hall simultaneously.

In a corner of the hall The Major Angel was busy moving a huge silver container across the floor. It was an old fashioned trunk with a hinged lid. As he opened it, he stooped on one knee and invited them to look. The inside was lined with shelves that began to move and grow as she surveyed the shoes to make her selection. There were: wonder shoes, slippers, moccasins, slides, loafers, toe shoes, high heels, wedges, work boots, snow boots, water shoes, golf shoes, and football cleats all in rows by size and color. Maybe there were sixty pairs or ninety thousand.

Beryle reached in and selected a pair of ballet slippers with pink satin ribbons. As she held them the ribbons became a gossamer-like filmy substance, consistent with foil, only pliable.

She thought, *I can make some wings of the ribbons and look like the Winged-footed Mercury.*

At the thought, the shoes left her hand and adjusted themselves comfortably on her feet. She twirled around for a while amazed that she could execute a few difficult ballet moves. Her toes and ankles did not hurt. When she stopped, she took them off, very carefully and admired the pink satin ribbon wings. She did not want to wear them; she just wanted to have them.

Have you ever heard a hush?

She heard the sound of a hush, as if a large wind had blown open a very large door to a large great room and all the large air went out. The sound was deafening. It caused her to shake her head, trying to make sense of the hush.

It became clear to her that they were inside **ETERNITY.**

It was gaping with vastness, hollow and forever – grand and resplendent and is.

Is?

IS NOW, ALWAYS WAS AND EVERMORE SHALL BE.

Is this what the Kingdom of God looks like?

"The Kingdom of God has been described, illustrated, likened unto and rightfully so. It, too, is a hologram of which this is just one pixel. Eternity is the great forever at your feet. It marks every beginning of every journey you take. When that journey is over you are at the beginning of the Forever Eternity to begin again." God told them.

Ah ha! She got it. The whole idea of life is one grand beginning never to end. She wanted to put that into perspective because she knew she needed to be able to teach it. *Wow! Here I am standing in the middle of Eternity wearing the Power of Love as a garment with winged shoes in my hand – thinking about teaching the Kingdom of God.*

The Major Angel spoke, *"They are Generational Shoes. They will not wear out. They were made in the Dry-Shod Factory. They are hand me downs. They have been handed down to you from your other generations. Wear them in the Kingdoms. There are Kingdoms of Ignorance and Kingdoms of Darkness through which you will see light and life. When you have to walk through darkness and ignorance use them. They can be your directional signals, cleats, boots, sandals, and track shoes. This pair of shoes is a gift. Think about them when your feet and your mouth do not match."*

The Place of Your Own Purpose

Her thought not to wear the shoes, but to carry them was interrupted when the sound of bells filled the space in her head that was thinking.

A giant ball of warm soft light appeared, rolling behind them, so huge that it engulfed the five of them. Inside the light were individual hammock-like seats in which they were swinging, as the ball moved along.

They sailed out past the Theatre, past the Mirrored Kingdom Hall into the vastness of forever. They had a forever ride. They were still, Eternity was moving. In Eternity all things possible, are seen. The things that are not possible are seen as though they are.

They saw unborn generations, unwritten books, songs unsung, portraits unpainted, buildings yet to be constructed, and civilizations to disappear. They saw an unpredictable exposure to the fields of all possibilities – just there – available for those who hear and want to live the higher laws.

"The urgency of wanting to know will propel you into the high part of yourself. There is an intrinsic goodness, right thinking-ness in everyone. You are born with it. It is called LOVE. It operates in babies. Watch how they give it away so freely. That is their natural state. It is trained out of them and replaced with ideas of fear, mistrust, suspicion and prejudice. The highness in humans can be developed so readily with just the premise of Love." That Voice was almost far away.

She wanted to think about what the Major Angel said. There was a distinct difference between the Voice of God and of the Major Angel, yet they sounded the same. She knew she did not have to think about the differences right then. Deep inside her thought processing system, there was a soft idea that they might be getting to the end of the tour and then what???

The change came when she heard the melody to the spiritual <u>"I Got Shoes"</u>. *She thought I will give my shoes to whomever so that she/he will not have to wait to get to heaven to put them on.* She had never thought of teaching lessons as the giving away of shoes. *The lessons are protective coverings to sustain the students over rocky places, through the mud of confusion, the pain of disappointment – even the fear of death.* Those thoughts seemed so heavy.

A very far away Voice spoke in an almost whisper, *"This is the Place of the Higher Law. This is the think room where decisions are made – not the 'should I' decisions but the' I will' decisions. During times when the whole of your world has turned against you, you might be too afraid to think past yes or no.*

"This is when you put on your shoes and walk all over God's heaven that is inside you. All situations are created by

you in your God Factory, in God's Perfection. Your response determines the shipping costs. Let your shoes be the directional signals. They will take you back to Kansas and into your bed.

"The height of the law is in your own reality. You determine how long you go to law school, when you are graduated; when you practice. Your reality will determine how honorably you will regard the Place of the Higher Law."

You

When the ball of light stopped each of them was deposited in the foyer of a sprawling Great Room. There was a splendid long table; oval and glistening, surrounded with padded high back chairs. The one heavy, strong taller chair at the head place was shaped the same as the others. At each place there was a place card. Beryle knew she was to be seated at the table, so she ambled up to it.

Each place card was blank until she looked at it – then her hologram appeared on it. If she passed it, it went blank again. There was no doubt that she belonged in the huge seat. It moved away from the table as she approached it. That did not surprise her because everything else inside God was automatic. As she took her place, the chair moved toward the table to make her comfortable.

Each seat around the table was occupied by an image of her. They were the same images she saw in the Mirrored Hall. Ha!

It seemed reasonable. There was no awe, no be quiet, you might be in the wrong chair. She was where she needed to be.

Having been in the Theater and having seen all the people she ever knew and would ever meet forever, there was one piece missing. What was the purpose? Why was she born? There had to be a complete equation including the total.

As she sat there and toyed with the idea of calling the meeting to order, she remembered a time when she was thirty-one – (that was a very good year). She was working as a recreational therapist in a local hospital, acute care psychiatric unit. That was a far cry from what she had in mind for her life's work – although she had no formal plans for her life's work then.

She had asked her mother how she could find a definite "what" for her life. Her mother told her to fast and pray.

"Ask God to show you why He made you."

Beryle remembered praying, "Now God, I want You to show me why You made me, please, and make sure I know it is You and don't fool me, Sir."

After that qualified prayer she lay down in her bed and decided that if God wanted to tell her He could wake her up. She did not know how long she was asleep – she just remembered sitting straight up in the bed wide awake.

She saw an image of herself at the foot of the bed – just standing. She spoke out loud (or maybe not) and said, "God I see that. What do You want me to say?"

The image began moving arms with hand gestures as if teaching and illustrating. Again, out loud (or maybe not), "I see that, God, what do You want me to do?"

"SHAKE MY PEOPLE AND WAKE THEM UP."

The figure faded and she lay down and went back to sleep. That was a hallmark in her life and it substantiated the ever present urge to teach.

The Teacher Beryle was seated in the first chair on the right, she put her Bible was on the table.

At ages eight and ten she and Dorothy knew about Broadway productions. Their mother would buy crepe paper for costumes for their Broadway Company. Beryle would write the plays and speeches. Charles Bettis would make up the dances. They staged the performances at Mr. Talbert's house in the basement where there was a concrete protrusion, perfect for a stage. The neighborhood kids never seemed to have nickels necessary to see the productions. That might be what put the Corsigan Sisters out of business.

When their older half brother, Emmett, would come to town he always had a nickel to see the play. It was usually such short notice that she could not get the troupe together. She would charge him the nickel, tell him the play and act out her part.

Being Beryle kept her busy as a young child. No doubt it kept her mother on her knees. The minor actress was seated, second chair on the left

Between ages four and five was her "paper period." If anyone in the house had a letter sized paper, unattached and blank on one side, it was fair game for the "book" she was writing. Her father had shown her how to poke a hole in the papers with a pencil. She would poke two holes on the left sides of the papers and tie a string through the holes. That made the raw material for her book. It was a book eternal, always with her and she was always writing in it.

At four she could not write cursive, nor could she print. She would copy things from the other sides of the papers and fill in the rest with scribble. If anyone had the time to listen, she would read him her story.

It was about her imaginary best friend, Beetabo. His life consisted of things she did not want to tell "them." If they would listen to the whole story, she would allow Beetabo to tell the test stuff. Beetabo told only the things that were not secret. The Author appeared and placed an unfinished copy of Ode to Beetabo on the table.

Since she was having the meeting and hearing various reports from the individuals who had lived life for her, the shape of her purpose was beginning to emerge.

All of her childhood led to an awareness and sensitivity that something was going on inside her. The fact was she never did belong nor could she do the group thing. She was not a very good team member. The young girl was fearlessly articulate, and had a flair for letting people know.

Her sweet maternal grandmother called her Bunchie. The best part of visiting grandma was when she got to read from their special book: Reader's Digest. Each time the cover was the same but the reading was new. She was in the third grade and it was o.k. that she could not pronounce all the words. She read with flair and excitement and made up the words she could not sound out. Those were good times. Her grandmother would listen with uninterrupted devotion to everything. Beryle even told her precious grandmother some of her secrets.

One day, after a secret telling episode, the grandmother said, "Bunchie, don't be so quick to give your opinion away. Some day you might need it. You always keep your sweet ways because they will take you places your money won't take you."

Bunchie was at the table, third seat on the right.

The mother-Beryle was there. When the pregnancy tricked her into labor, she was through with being pregnant **FOREVER.**

She just knew her overdue baby would have long flowing hair. That was a secret. As often as she could, during the tiresome pregnancy, she ate tangerines. Tangerines make babies have long hair. That was a fact. She had heard it in the prenatal clinic waiting room from a girl expecting her third longhaired baby.

When she got to the hospital, it never crossed her mind that Dorothy could not go to the labor room with her. Back then, visitors were not allowed. (Her husband, Steve, was in the military.) She was surprised and scared, but most of all disappointed that Dorothy could not be with her. The elevator had a window in the door and Dorothy's big blue-green eyes were filled with tears as her face disappeared.

Beryle had secret. She had a little comb and brush set in a blue lace drawstring bag in her right armpit. The little hairbrush had a silver backing on it – the little comb did, too. It was tricky to keep it hidden. In the delivery room, one person on her right was saying, "push", on the left, someone kept yelling, "breathe slowly and pant."

The pain kept coming and coming and she kept hurting and hurting.

She stopped breathing.

She stopped pushing.

She needed to think, she thought, *Nobody can hurt this bad and be alive so I must be dead.*

She shifted into a "dead mode" and went limp –and the baby oozed out.

Everybody was smiling and there was awe... waiting. Then, the cry and they began to say nice things congratulating her. She had her eyes closed, because she was dead. She came back to life because the hairbrush was digging into her rib cage.

The sight of that upside down baby covered with placental issue was too much. Beryle, the new mother, began to cry and sob in abject grief. She could not get her breath; she was retching. Blood pressure shot up – they needed to know why the sudden shift.

At that point the baby's back was still facing her and she did not know its gender. She just had to have a boy. There was no way a girl would fit into her plans. Girls needed too many things: pocketbooks and ribbons and dolls and the endless hair combing. Hair combing was the real reason that the baby had to be a boy. After all, she had this comb and brush set and baby boys with long hair were stylish.

A nurse said, "Tell her what it is." The doctor, holding the baby, turned it around to her. What she saw was a red, engorged face, a body covered with placental issue and turquoise testicles.

She shrieked– "He's baldheaded!"

Places In God

    The expectant mother had been to natural childbirth classes, new in the area, and she was the first one in her class to deliver. That got her a case presentation in the amphitheater, at the hospital. The maternity interns attended to hear her case history and more importantly, to hear her "he's baldheaded" story.

    The nurses dubbed him, "Little Baldheaded Prince." During her stay they called her "The Queen of Hair". The little comb and brush set, in a light blue lace drawstring pouch, was on the table where the new mother sat.

    Across from her, the Beryle of determination walked in, sat down and put a single key on the table. It was a key to her first apartment.

    She and Darryl were living with her mother and her recent husband, Mr. Hall who had a few issues with Beryle. The baby's crying kept him from sleeping. Guess who would drink the baby's milk. That meant she had to walk to the open all night drug store to buy milk. The clerk would save milk for her and listen to why she was out at night with such a young baby. One time Beryle put cod liver oil in the milk. She never had to walk to the drug store again.

    The new mother would get up around 5:00a.m., bathe and feed Darryl, wash his clothes and diapers, hang them out on the line and go back to bed. Ms. Hall would come at her, "Get up. You look lazy. It's morning, get up." Useless explanation of all the work Beryle had done did not help.

    One morning in May, Ms. Hall was yelling for the new mother to get up. She jumped up with fire in her eyes. That was the day. Even if she had to sleep in a canoe, in the river, under

117

a bridge, with a tent over the canoe, she had all she could take. She got her baby up and got them dressed and walked from East 65th Street down to East 30th Street where the Administrative Offices were for government housing.

A Mr. Mays told her he had a two-year waiting list which was closed and he was not adding names at that time.

The next morning they were up and out before Ms. Hall could even think to talk to or about them. Mr. Mays told her the same thing without even looking up to see her. The third morning she had bus fare. She and Darryl and Mr. Mays got off the same bus. She chatted with him along the way to his office.

She went in behind him and sat down, with her baby, until he was ready for business. He told her he still had a waiting list two years long.

"Please look to see if somebody moved out yesterday. That would make one apartment available and take one person off the list and make one space on the list and you could put me on."

He said, "No."

The next morning and the next, skip Saturday/Sunday, Monday she and Darryl went to his office. On the eighth encounter, even before she could ask him if anyone had moved yet, he grunted, "Can you bring me some identification and fifty-seven dollars?"

When she put the key on the table, the Beryle at the head of the table smiled at her.

One by one, images of her appeared and occupied the seats. When she thought about her eternal book, she thought about T.A. He was one of George's friends who went to jail. He kept sending letters to George asking him to visit and bring cigarettes. George would not go.

The newlywed Beryle decided to write to him. It was a note tucked in the mail that turned out to be a full-blown letter that was sent once a week for ten years. During that time she got Thomas to read books, to learn to play chess and to keep a journal. She sent him postcards from all her travels. The letter writer came in and put a pen and envelope on the table.

The fashion model bopped in with her portfolio. She was a Pixie type who stole shows with her personality and antics on stage. Back in those days models were allowed to be people with clothes on. The modeling opened the door for the trips to Paris, London, Madrid, Lisbon, Rome, Venice, Milan, and Florence. It was exciting, fun and hard work.

What began as a table with empty chairs grew longer with new seats available as other Beryles showed up. Each one had a story to tell about those things that shaped her life.

There was one who organized a Conga line in a roof garden night club in Madrid, Spain. After she started it, she began to encourage the patrons to get up and dance. When she grabbed the arm of a stately old gentleman, seated with a younger man, the young man jumped to his feet and pronounced, "Madam, Do-Not-Touch-Him-He-Is-A-Duke!!!"

Beryle kept dancing right there at the table, still holding the older gentleman's arm. "Duke, Smuke, Come on and dance!!"

The Duke was delighted. He got up and joined in the line behind her. He seemed to be coming away from feeble as he placed his hands firmly around her waist.

He followed her carefully and laughed out loud. He threw his head back turning it from side to side. She led the conga line up onto the band stand and in through the kitchen. When it was over, Duke Smuke told her he was grateful to her. That was the best holiday he ever had. He wanted to dance the night away but his station in life would not allow it.

When the night ended, Beryle decided not to think of an international incident. The dancing model took a seat and rested her giant portfolio on the floor.

Beryle called the meeting to order. "You are here, inside of God, to join together all these in a holy matrimony. This is not to be entered into lightly. You have been courting each other for years. You came here because you were looking for something. You were looking for union. Whomever you are and whatever you do, you are part of a fragmented whole. This union is necessary before you can see God. Take hands with the aspects of personality seated on either side of you.

Do you take these other parts of you to be your whole you, to live together as one, presenting a single image at all times, to get along with one another, not in subjugation; but harmony, to live together in one body, developing a single is-ness in health and in wealth so that you – all can live?"

They all said, "I do" and dissolved into the Beryle at the head of the disappearing table.

The Issue of God

When the table and the many personality images disappeared, she felt like she was tempered. Where did that idea come from? She thought about her clay robin in kindergarten. It had been tempered. All her parts had been joined together to secure them in their right places, like colors added to clay so they will not run or fade. The tempering locked her personhood in place. It let her know that in God there are no mistakes. Not one of the things she ever did was judged or criticized.

Coming inside of God was a designated organized time for her to make friends with herself. Everything in God was about her. She learned ALL God has is hers.

When Beryle was a child she knew about a god who had to be obeyed and pleased. He needed to be begged, never to be understood and most surely never to be heard – except when it was thundering. It took her over fifty years to ideate a God she could visit.

Reality arrived as she found herself floating along in her thoughts about a God she could visit...*I am not talking about*

121

the church god. I divorced him long ago. I needed to know the God that is ALL ENERGY. It seemed reasonable to me that the same ENERGY that sets the seasons and, puts those incredible colors on tropical fish, must know me. I am part of that Energy? Why can I not know that I am?

The table was gone. She was standing in His Higherness wearing her Power of Love garment with her Generational shoes in her hand. She knew it was time to leave. Her head was full of unutterable things. How could she describe the exquisiteness of Places in God where she had lived all of her life? Just imagine being invited to go on a tour inside of Eternity to look back and see your everything even before it happened. That is the Issue of God extended to every creature:

BE STILL AND KNOW THAT (who is the,) I AM GOD. IT IS YOU.

The Omega

"The Phoenix and the Major Angel guided and directed you to some of the Places in Me. There is what is known as 'many mansions' inside my body. That is a generic term designed to entertain those who are not willing to exert the effort to experience the mansions. You saw people in the Obedience corridor stuck to the walls. Because you chose to follow on to know, I will show you to a Place you have not been. It is a Place past letting go. In order to get there you had to yield to All Truth. You decided to buy a ticket.

*"Do you remember being willing to give up <u>everything</u> you knew for that which you did not know? When you heard the idea, the first time you were neither hesitant nor resistant. You did it. That is not to say 'everything' was much. Your **everything** was the price of the ticket.*

"You knew how to chomp and claw, how to get them told and how to assert your rightness. You could flirt and con your way into the hearts and minds of those you encountered. You could sing and dance on your own self made portable stage, as

eternal entertainment, for whomever, without tax or charge. You had your own comedy dog and pony show and could flush out tears at a moment's notice.

"Perhaps you get the gist of 'all you knew.' Does it surprise you that you were readily willing to give that up? No part of what you knew is being judged. Each part served you; you were masterful at the art of being Beryle. You rarely made attempts to make major changes.

"The admirable part is that you were good at it. You knew that you knew, even though much of it was not in cement. That is why it was so easy for you to part with it. Moreover, all of it had been used, and often. You were fiercely familiar with most of it. Some of it you kept in reserve and you would spring it on folks - and surprise both you and them.

"The Place you are going is far away beyond where you would have any use for the things you gave up. You were willing to have them replaced with that which you did not know.

"I invited you, then, into Places in God, inside Me. Had you kept your old ways, you would not be here NOW. Can you see that NOW is who I AM and who you are?

"It is gravely important (enjoy the word) that you bury the past and move on. As you separate yourself from your former mentality, do so with abandoned joy.

"Nothing can compare with where you are going; with what you will know and experience. If you are ready... we can proceed.

"First you must <u>HEAR</u> and <u>SEE</u> an idea. Explore this instruction carefully. Hear and See. Release and Allow. That

is the same as what you call 'Letting Go.' You cannot let go of something you will not see.

"If you cannot see that someone does not want to be in a relationship with you, if there is pain you cannot get past the pain. As you continue to revisit the pain you encapsulate the idea and cannot let it go. The capsule hides it from your sight.

"In the Place where you are going, you must let go. Let go of: (you fill in the blank) Hurts, Grudges, Items, Bills, Animals, Family (dead and alive) Houses, Accounts, New and Old Debts. You get the idea??? I told you, you will have to hear and see ideas in this Place.

"Take a seat. Sit quietly and reduce the noise level of the internal dialogue. That is the way to relax your mind. As you release your mental muscles the old ideas can slip through to the Exit of Intent. Can you see what will happen? As you begin this clear hearing you will cause ideas to come into sight. When they are seen they can be dismissed. Hear one idea, see it, scoot it away. Drop it over into the Universal Solvent, called the Sea of Forgetfulness where it will be remembered no more by you or Me.

"This may take some stretching. You have come this far.
"Think!!!!

"How will your life be when you engage in this new Place? This idea is not new to you. You have been told:

"Let It Go
"Let It Out
"Let it Alone

"Let It Be, yet you kept it. Your willingness brought you here – inside of Me. The Idea was to show you You – to cause you to think of yourself as you <u>and</u> to think of Me as you.

"With this simple instruction, the two of us can become one and you will be ready. Breathe and reflect the instruction: LET IT GO.

*"Now that all of you are one, joined together at the table in the Great Room, allow yourself to <u>release</u> and <u>allow</u>. As you inhale the <u>release</u> and exhale the <u>allowing</u>, you will float on the breathing into **<u>The Place of Effortlessness</u>**.*

"The movement of the air requires no effort on your part. When you push the willingness button the passing away happens with no help from you. Your part is to want to be there. It is called dwelling ...'secret place of the most High.' You already know how to do that, instinctively. In this Place you can ...'mount up with wings as eagles, you can run and not be weary, walk and not faint.' There is neither time nor space nor gravity in this Place. Embrace the Effortlessness Place with joy.

"This is the End and the Beginning of Places in God."

…Said The Author….

(Comments made at her seventy fifth birthday celebration.)

Thank you for coming to help to celebrate my birthday. As I look back, some of the years are missing. Somewhere they are all jammed together. They arrived in sequential order with sobering regularity. I greeted each one with appropriate acknowledgement, as I was able. In my younger days the excitement of a new year did not register as I was busy on the mark, getting set to go. By the time I heard the starter pistol, some of them had run off and left me. I tried to catch them but that was useless.

I could ask along with you, where did the years go? Or, I could think, the years bring life to me. They brought me a wonder for nature, a love for animals, a fearless curiosity and, oh yes, a love of music.

I remember being awarded a ribbon for my school because I had the highest score, in the whole city. Elementary school children were bused to Severance Hall to classical concerts. The orchestra was behind closed curtains. The children were tested with the curtains closed and required to identify each instrument by sound.

Schools required much of my energy because I was always organizing, inventing or creating something. That marked me, at least, and I feel certain I marked them, too.

The years watched me and I did not watch them. They saw me step into motherhood with the grace of an arriving albatross.

By the time I figured out how to fly, I did not need to. They encouraged me to find a place in life where I could be me. That was a major challenge.

I went through six passports. Our church took a Caribbean cruise. We went to Australia and we took a ride on the Queen Mary 11. I went to Key West, Florida to swim with the dolphins. My sister, Dorothy and I went to China to see the Terracotta Army. I climbed up the Great Wall four thousand feet. Two ladies and I rented a car in Frankfort, Germany where I got a chance to drive on the famed Autobahn over 175 kilometers an hour, in the rain, mind you.

Ask Dorothy about the time I rented a store front to house donations to raise money for me to go to the Olympic Games in Japan. One time I started up a radio broadcast that was a monumental flop. I lost a few dollars in the stock market. I called myself investing in an investment company and got took!!! I modeled professionally for fifteen years. I traveled across the USA with a research team of Medical Record Technicians, trained at the Center for Disease control in Atlanta, Ga.

Then there were the years I managed to sponsor retreats and teach Bible classes. I was on the invitational preaching circuit for a few years before becoming a Pastor. In my early adulthood I was an actress at the famous Karamu Theater, in Cleveland. Somewhere in those years I did stand-up comedy, before it was popular for girls to do. I had a few miscellaneous employment experiences, from which people seemed to enjoy firing me. I managed to survive.

The years brought my husband, George into my life. Those years were not swift nor did they fly by. They seemed to mark time so that we could enjoy them.

Child hood, student hood, employee-hood, neighborhood, all the hoods and hats I managed to wear, brought you to me. Some of you I have known forever and some of you just caught up with the years that brought you to me.

However, when ever, whatever or whomever, we made it. You have seen me grow from a long legged, curious, noisy little girl through seventy five years. Many of you hooked in at twenty, even earlier. For those of you who met me in the later life, after my cocoon stage, you found a butterfly trying her wings, flitting all over the place.

Perhaps you saw me in your office or your place of business, even in your living room, at a meeting or in a church. It might have been on a trip to a faraway place or in a swimming pool. You may have been a consumer of one of the many products I offered. Most of you know I am a seller of goods.

I sent the years away for them to return to me – and they did. They returned and brought you to me, here and now. Have they been good years? Yes and No. They brought some pain and sorrow, a few bumps and detours but for the most part I have had a good ride.

Skeletons in the closet; I have a few. You, who know about them, please be kind. I have experienced a very full, rich seventy five years. My garden is filled with the beauty of your very personal individual blossoms and fragrances. I cherish each of you. It took some doing but we got it done. Seventy five more; not a chance!!! "Dying is easy. It's the hell they serve for breakfast that is hard." (Author unknown) When you go around and do it right, once is enough.

Again, thank you for being here.

About the Author

This celebrated teacher is Pastor of Spiritual Growth Ministries in Cleveland, Ohio. She shares a depth of wisdom, talent, humor and a growing appreciation for those things spiritual. Her panoramic imagination stretches beyond preconceived human boundaries, in a voice that is easy to be trusted.

Her travels have taken her to five continents, several tropical islands and to all but four of the lower forty-eight states, to teach and to be taught. Her passion is teaching which she does with unique quality and enthusiasm. She is widowed, mother of one son, Darryl. They live together in Twinsburg, Ohio, which she says is in the woods, but not in the country.

PLACES IN GOD is a delicate adventure that transposes a manner of wisdom into learning entertainment. It leads the reader on an allegorical journey through the inside of God's body. The Major Angel, God's tour guide, escorts five students into His ears and through His heart with stopovers in His attitudes and freedoms. They went to a boutique, a theatre and they sat in a boardroom.

With excitement and awe they were absorbed. With breathtaking silent transports, to and through phenomenal inner parts, they were literally digested and released. There is a spiritual increase that becomes apparent as you are propelled with them through PLACES IN GOD.